CONSPIRACY OF SILENCE

CONSPIRACY OF SILENCE

Religious and Patriarchal Roots of Violence Towards Women

SPENCER A. MURRAY, D. MIN

Cover designed by Robin Locke Monda
Author Photo Credit: Clarence Gabriel Photography

Printed in the United States of America
First Edition
ISBN-13 978-0-578-50842-9

In memory of my mother, Vivian E. Murray, who despite being subject to the perils of patriarchy, always managed to display the love, grace and sacrifice that mirrored the face of God; my father, Milton L. Murray, Sr., whose brief presence in my life shaped me into the man I am today; and to the late Reverend Dr. Joan Speaks, whose guidance, love and friendship inspired me to make Conflict Transformation a way of life. I stand on the shoulders of each of you.

TABLE OF CONTENTS

FOREWORD

A T THE TIME that I wrote this foreword, it was a little over three years since Spence said those few words to me that forever changed how I see him, other men and even *myself*. It was a random weekday afternoon. I was sitting on one side of our bed and Spence was sitting on the other. He said, "Erica, I am sorry. On behalf of any man that has hurt you, violated you, not given you what you needed and deserved, I am sorry. I stand in the gap to say what other men couldn't—didn't. I'm sorry."

A couple of years earlier, Spencer started working on his dissertation around Conflict Transformation for the New York Theological Seminary. Neither of us was familiar with the concept of Conflict Transformation prior to his enrollment. Little did we know that his decision to pursue his doctorate in this area of study would powerfully influence the trajectory of our lives. He narrowed his focus to the ways in which patriarchy, rooted in religious dogma, serves as the foundation for the perpetuated subjugation of women, which ultimately leads to physical, psychological and emotional violence.

The #MeToo Movement, started by Tarana Burke, became more pronounced after the likes of Alyssa Milano and Gabrielle Union took it on in Hollywood, creating an increased awareness and sensitivity to the concept of male privilege. For women, the outrageous benefits of male privilege are not new. An impetus to the movement began in 1991 when Professor Anita Hill pushed back against Clarence Thomas' unwelcomed sexual advances and harassment, during his Supreme Court Justice nomination hearing. As more women recall, rename and reclaim their power, and no longer ignore and blindly accept the notion of "boys will be boys," we will continue to witness the walls of silence crumbling down while a new, sustainable level of consciousness arises. We are witnessing a heightened momentum of social change that is also visible in racial and political divides. It has found its way into business boardrooms, sporting events, coffee shops and our homes. Yet, the church has been fairly *silent*.

The body of work in the subsequent pages is the result of countless hours of research, studies, surveys, workshops and conversations. What was not anticipated is the transformation that I have had the opportunity to witness as Spence has evolved into the man that he is today. His work around male privilege and toxic masculinity has changed the shape and formation of his thoughts and ideas, as well as how he shows up in the world–as evidenced by his apology to me. As he stood as a vessel for the men of my past, I saw and, more importantly, I felt and knew that he really was *seeing* me. All of us want *to be seen*. Highlight that word in your mind—*seen*—because what comes with being seen by another, especially someone that we love, is an unspoken appreciation for you as a person. You deserve to be witnessed to and heard simply because you exist. Today, our relationship, appreciation and love for one another is stronger, relevant and freeing.

While witnessing Spence's transformation, I underwent my own shift in awareness. You see, in order for patriarchy and male privilege to survive, we as women have to buy into it as our reality. One of my favorite quotes by Eleanor Roosevelt says, "No one can make you feel inferior without your consent." Said differently, patriarchy, male privilege and toxic masculinity cannot exist without women agreeing to its essence and supporting its existence–even if it is through our complicit silence that many of us have embraced as part of our religious upbringing. I gave myself permission to acknowledge, forgive and release any lingering ideas that I held for Spence as my protector, financier and anything else that kept him tethered to religious and socially accepted definitions of manhood.

This book is laid out differently from what you may be used to since it is the byproduct of Spencer's dissertation. Since Conflict Transformation starts with revealing how the interpretation of one's stories and experiences gives way to conflict in their life, he starts with a highly personal and genuinely transparent look into his childhood relationships with his parents. He highlights the lessons that he took from each of his parents and how they impacted the way he showed up in his friendships, as well as romantic relationships. I imagine that the heart it took for him to share his own story will allow other men—and the women who love them—to see their own stories more clearly.

As you read the pages that follow, allow yourself to experience a personal, intellectual and spiritual journey, which may cause you to question ideas and beliefs you have previously accepted. Give yourself permission to be open to new, unique ideas that are beyond labels like gender, religion and race. Behold an appreciation for a deeper love of humanity.

In deep love and gratitude,
Erica Parks Murray

PREFACE

WRITING THIS BOOK proved to be challenging for me. The difficulty in writing it reveals just how damaging patriarchy can be on the psyche. I've been ingrained with a form of manhood that cautions me from revealing my own warped ideas about masculinity. A large part of me feels as if I'm breaking a code of silence–worthy of being kicked out of the *man club*. Another part of me feels shame and conviction as I realize that my masculine indoctrination caused me to enact certain forms of emotional and psychological violence against women, in addition to being silently complicit in other forms of violence. After all the work I've done in this area, I still have a high degree of trepidation when it comes to putting my story on paper. It is easy for me to talk about what "the experts" have said about patriarchy. With ease, I can put the recent rash of sexual assault accusations into context and talk about the actions men must take to put an end to the violence that women face at the hands of men. And, on a regular basis, I even speak to men about the toxic masculinity that has kept us emotionally imprisoned. However, when it comes to talking about the roots of toxic masculinity in my own life, it becomes much more difficult. For me to give an honest, authentic account of my own indoctrination into manhood, I'll have to reveal things about myself and my family - my father particularly - that are not so flattering.

With all that said, I remain committed to a healing that calls for me to uncover the things I've kept hidden for far too long. I often suggest to people that they cannot heal what they won't reveal. Therefore, I know that before I can provide a pathway to healing for others, I must heal *myself*. When it comes to the issue of violence against women, I must explore the probability that my propensity to enact violence upon women first manifested from the violence I enacted upon myself.

For many men, violence toward *self* is often a direct result of masculine indoctrination—a phenomenon that I'll explore throughout this book.

For the benefit of my healing, as well as the healing of other men, I'll do my best to reveal what I consider to be the root causes of the violence that keep men imprisoned—violence that all too often is directed at the women in their lives. I realize that, at best, I can only speak for myself. This is my journey. However, I suspect that this journey is not mine alone.

In 2012, I was charged with the task of identifying a subject that I wanted to explore for my dissertation. I decided to explore the issue of physical, emotional and psychological violence toward women. I realized how blind I had been to this subject in the past. If you ask most men about their role in the proliferation of domestic and sexual violence against women, they would probably argue that they have had nothing to do with the issue. Many would even argue that the problem belongs to the women who are victimized before they would address the men who do the victimizing. In fact, most men fail to see how they impact the issue at all. These same men absolve themselves by asserting that they have never hit, raped or sexually assaulted a woman.

I know this to be true because I was one of those men. I had to acknowledge the possibility that my *male privilege* blinded me from seeing the problem. I heard of the term *privilege* before, but only in racial contexts when *white privilege* was highlighted. And just as some of my white counterparts had to come to grips with their white privilege, I painfully had to come face-to-face with the privilege of being male. I was so accustomed to the notion of white privilege that I failed to see the privilege I lived with every day. My privilege afforded me the opportunity to push the issue off on someone else. It pains me deeply to say that, at that time, I concluded that if it wasn't happening to me or anyone I knew personally—and if I wasn't the perpetrator—there was little I could do besides offer my heartfelt sympathy to the victims of such crimes. I never considered that my silence made me a complicit agent in these atrocities against women. If I was in any way complicit, I had to explore all the reasons for my complicity. The last thing I wanted to consider was that I was, *or had ever been*, a violent man.

It was time to consider differently.

ACKNOWLEDGMENTS

A N ENDEAVOR SUCH as this is never completed without the support of friends, family, and those who contribute their expertise to the final product. If any names were forgotten on this page, charge it to my head and not my heart. My ultimate intent is for my life to reflect gratitude in a way that words alone cannot express. There are specific people, however, whose mentioning is well-deserved.

First, I express my enduring gratitude for Dr. Marcia Riggs and the late Reverend Dr. Joan Speaks, who recognized the power of transformation in me and recruited me to the doctoral program at New York Theological Seminary—a seminary that remains committed to urban ministry in the real world. A special thanks is reserved for Dr. Wanda Lundy of NYTS, for her ardent support and endless supply of grace. Your faith in me never wavered. And to my Conflict Transformation cohorts, the Reverend Dr. Nathaniel Dunlap and Camille Turner-Townsend—my heartfelt thanks. Your presence continues to transform my life.

The original dissertation, which this book is based on, could not have been born without the love and support of a team who believed in me, challenged me, and held me accountable. Thank you to my entire Site Team: Reverend Shaheerah Stephens, whose journey heavily inspired the writing of the dissertation; Naomi Khalil for always being totally and unconditionally committed to my success; Dr. Ollie Johnson for setting forth an initial vision for this project; and Dr. Vera Stenhouse, whose commitment and dedication single-handedly led to the completion of the dissertation. With you, I share the fruits of this project.

There are many who contributed their love, time, and energy to the development of my dissertation. Transforming Love Community, my Detroit church family: thank you for transforming me by your unconditional love and for always being the wind beneath my wings. To the men of Transforming Love: I salute you for your courage, transparency and willingness to share your stories with me for the ultimate transformation of all men. Spirit and Truth Sanctuary, my Decatur church family: thank you for your inclusive love, acceptance and the invitation to keep evolving. Thanks also goes to the men of Spirit and Truth for your presence and willingness to redefine what it means to be a man. And to my brothers who gave of their time to complete the dissertation survey: thank you for your service, loyalty and desire for us all to become healthy and whole men.

I also extend a special thanks to Pastor D.E. Paulk, Lori Robinson, Carole Hoover-Battle and Reverend Shaheerah for trusting me enough to share your individual journeys. Your words and stories will provide healing for those in need.

I am tremendously thankful for those who added their expertise to the dissertation and the subsequent formation of this book. Tom Fuller, much appreciation for your commitment to making the original dissertation look good. You are a miracle worker. Likewise, it takes more than one set of eyes to review a book manuscript. Thank you Pastor Clariece Paulk, LaDonna Diaz, and Rodara Nelloms for your willingness to provide further clarity and editing to the book. Regardless of the size of your contribution, it does not go unnoticed. I am most thankful for my final editor, Tenita Chantilly Johnson, CEO & Founder of So It Is Written Writing & Editing Services. Your professionalism, expert editing, unwavering support and patience is unmatched. Your dedication helped give me the final push I needed. I am also exceedingly grateful for Robin Locke Monda, who felt my vision from the very beginning and created a cover design that speaks volumes. And to Phillip Gessert: thank you for formatting the final product. You helped bring it all together.

Nothing worthwhile is ever created in a vacuum. I am blessed and forever grateful for my loving and supportive family. You all have given me the greatest gift by sharing your lives with me—particularly my brother, Hamilton A. Murray. Thank you for demonstrating the power of transformation and always striving to be a better brother. Special thanks as well to my cousin, Judith A. Murray, for always modeling what a strong, transformed woman looks like. Aunt Joya, thank you for inspiring me with your lifelong commitment to freedom and justice. To Ray C. Johnson—thank you for the years of loyal friendship and guidance. Your commitment to The Mission continues to inspire mine. And to the dynamic Nichole Christian, many thanks to you for inspiring me to put all of myself into the work. You were there from beginning to the end. And finally to my brothers of Kappa Alpha Psi Fraternity Inc.—thank you for the shared journey. May we continue to evolve from Kappa Men that love God, to Godly Men that love Kappa.

Above all, I want to thank and acknowledge my wife and inspiration to become a more loving and awakened man—Erica Parks Murray. Your love, support and sacrifice never goes unnoticed. Whatever I do on this planet, your presence increases its meaning exponentially.

INTRODUCTION

WHEN IT COMES to uncovering the roots of behavior, there is a difference between a reason and an excuse. There are valid reasons for thinking and acting the way that we do. Initially, and unbeknownst to us as children, we learn to think and act according to what is modeled for us by adults, peer groups and society. Later in life, it becomes helpful for us to revisit these origins in attempt to correct the perceptions that have caused tension in our lives. The act of uncovering the cause of our actions should encourage us to take responsibility for those actions. Once responsibility is taken, we should no longer use our prior perceptions as excuses for current and future behavior.

Much of this writing represents my honest attempt at identifying the early influences that shaped my idea of what it meant to be a man, a mate and a husband. Most importantly, I hope to reveal how my male indoctrination caused me to be oblivious to the pain of women—pain that I often caused when they became collateral damage in *my own* misguided pursuit of what it meant to be a man. As painful as it may be to reveal uncomfortable truths, I do it in hopes that other men will do the same. As for me, I hope to rid myself of the false truths that allowed me to use my *maleness* as an excuse for ignorance, and for contributing to a system that has historically disempowered women. Most importantly, I offer this writing in the spirit of reconciliation to the women I've known, as well as to those whom I don't know—all who were and are subjected to the perils of patriarchy. Through this reconciliation, may I become a more sensitive human being and a better mate to my wife, Erica.

During my studies for my dissertation project, I was required to identify a subject that would allow me to explore the tensions within the subject area, then use transformative tools to change the parties in tension. The transformation would build new platforms, which would allow the parties to relate in ways that would decrease violence and increase peace. What follows is my exploration of gender violence and what I see as some of the root causes. Most of the book is taken from my completed dissertation on the same subject. Because of the unfolding nature of my truth, my current thought process continues to evolve beyond what was written in the final version. Although much of what you'll read has religious overtones, the thoughts and opinions expressed are not solely applicable to religious-minded people. The religious focus of the writing was necessary for the seminary to which the project was submitted. I remain committed to the idea, however, that religion and the way we *imagine* God extends to virtually every area of our lives. With that being said, we can change the way we *live* and *love* by first changing the way we look at the *divine*.

I realized some time ago that it is impossible for me to engage in any type of transformative work without revealing my own journey of transformation. It was on rare occasion that someone *wasn't* interested in my motivations for embarking upon a study of violence toward women. It slowly dawned on me that my entire life had actually prepared me to tackle this subject matter.

In Chapter 1, I explore the roots of my perceptions; how those perceptions gave birth to my misconceptions about myself, women and relationships; and the journey that led me to the dawning of a new understanding.

Chapter 2 establishes a historical context for the intersection of religion and violence, and introduces gender violence as a direct consequence of patriarchal interpretations of God and Scripture. The chapter also recognizes male privilege as a byproduct of patriarchy and how that privilege creates standards that affirm men, while yet oppressing women.

Chapter 3 acquaints you with the prevalence of violence against women and gives a brief history of the Christian roots of that violence. The chapter uncovers the perverse attitudes and perceptions of women, and how they set the tone for the objectification and oppression of women. Biblical Scriptures are identified that give witness to the fact that women's bodies were not their own and considered expendable in the cause of religious conquests. This chapter illustrates how early church attitudes about women are still, not only adhered to today, but responsible for policies and actions that are violent toward them.

Chapter 4 introduces the concept of patriarchy and how it exists as the system that bestows a secondary status to women, while bestowing primary power and privilege to men. This privilege ensures that men essentially make, interpret and mete out justice according to standards they create.

The chapter also illustrates how patriarchy extends its reach into virtually every institution that our country holds dear.

Chapter 5 examines the way in which men are indoctrinated into masculinity. It reveals how the very process of indoctrination is one that puts men at odds with the feminine aspect of creation. The chapter further exposes how the unhealthy nature of masculine indoctrination causes many men to turn violence inward before directing it outward. Finally, you are invited to see how hyper masculinity, like patriarchy, creates power structures that breed violence and threaten to destroy the personhood of women.

Chapter 6 introduces Narrative Mediation as the framework used throughout the dissertation project to interpret the transformative experiences of project participants. While I did not include specific data, or the various methods used for gathering that data, it was profoundly apparent that Narrative Mediation was, and is, a highly effective transformative tool. The chapter continues by offering alternatives to defining God by a male construct only. Accompanied by an expanded definition of God, the chapter provides inclusive Scriptures and interpretations of Scripture that elevate and include women as original agents in the advancement of the Kingdom of God. In terms of relationships, the chapter proposes that the recognition of women's agency, along with their inherent right to exist equitably, will reduce the adversarial nature of relationships and create unions based on divine love, mutual respect and lasting peace.

Finally, Chapter 7 offers final thoughts on how this project has transformed my life and the implications it has for further healing in the community.

CHAPTER 1
EARLY INFLUENCES

I WAS RAISED by a controlling father and what I thought at the time, was a passive mother. While I was never specifically taught how to be a man, I took my cues from what I saw and heard at home, at school and in the neighborhood. In the process, my definition of what a man *was* often came from discovering what a man *wasn't*. From my surroundings, I learned that a man doesn't cry, whine or complain. I learned that a man *sucks it up* and never lets anyone see his emotions. I learned that a boy who wants to be *manlike* should be aggressive and never turn down an opportunity to be competitive with other boys. In my neighborhood and school, if you didn't join in on the games, or have some level of athletic skill, you were left out of the *boys' club*.

At home, my initial idea of manhood was defined by a father who was merely *present*. Up until the age of 17, my father was *the* commanding presence in the household. While many young boys would find comfort in that fact, oftentimes, I did not. In retrospect, I'm immensely grateful for the time I had with him. But, as a young boy, I found myself navigating his moods, as well as my own emotions, when he was around. I never knew what his mood was going to be. One moment, he could be relaxed and funny. The next moment, he could be angry and extremely critical. In my young mind, I translated his actions to mean that *I wasn't enough*—tough enough, man enough, or simply *just not enough*. Consequently, I often stayed out of his way. I thought if I made myself invisible, I would spare myself the hurt that often came with his words and the tone of his voice.

There weren't a lot of outward expressions of affection in my household. Outward expressions of love, happiness and joy were rarely a part of my daily experience. For the most part, love was expressed through the meeting of obligations and commitments. If you had a roof over your head, clothes on your back, and food on the table, then love was supposed to be understood. Of course, there were happy moments that accompanied holidays and such, but they often seemed like momentary celebrations that would soon cease. Often, these holidays were accompanied by their fair share of drinking. In fact, alcohol seemed to be a prerequisite for the varied emotions expressed by my parents. On one hand, alcohol would soften my mother a bit and allow her to express loving affections she wouldn't otherwise express. For my father, alcohol intensified his emotions and fueled his critical nature. Since this was often the case, I came to understand at a young age that my job was to be compliant, do what was expected of me, and have little or nothing at all to say about it. This information stayed with me and became part of my definition of manhood.

My mother, for the most part, was silent about the methods my father used to raise me and my brother. Many times, I could see that she was pained by what my father said and what he did. Every now and then, she raised an objection to my father. However, this was always done in what she thought was a private space—never deliberately in front of us.

There were times, though, when I would overhear her say, "Milton, you shouldn't say that to those boys!" or "Milton, you're being too hard on those boys!"

Each time, his basic response would be, "*Shut up, Vivian! I know what I'm doing*!"

His response would simply render her silent—silent and frustrated. It seemed that my mother's only recourse was to instill life lessons in her two boys, whenever possible. Church attendance was a mandatory way in which to instill those lessons, while also giving us a sense of something greater than ourselves and our situation. I've now come to believe that church was her way of coping and surviving, just as much as it was to instill a sense of God in us.

As the years went by, even after his passing, my resentment grew about the way I was raised. The way my mother was forced to be silently complicit in the oppression I felt at home. I began to question why we accepted his control. I questioned whether we should've accepted it at all. I often wondered how my life would've turned out differently if she had left him while we were young boys. I wondered what would've happened if I had raised a defiant voice to his need to control. Unfortunately, I knew very well what would've happened. I had a front row seat to witness what happened to my older brother when he attempted to defy my father's authority. One night, after heavy drinking, my father challenged my brother to a face-off punctuated with a push and a punch to the chest. It wasn't pretty, and I didn't want any part of that.

Consequently, my early ideas of men's and women's roles were gathered from my mother and father. From my father, I learned that being a man was about being present, disciplined, controlling and indifferent to how others felt about your methods of control. From my mother, I learned that being a woman was about sacrificing a piece of your soul for the sake of your family. From her, I learned how to be silent. From him, I learned how to use my presence as a means of control. From my mother, I learned how to use indifference to shield myself from pain. From my father, I learned that being a man was about obligations and responsibilities, not emotions. From my mother, I learned that a little alcohol could help lower inhibitions and create a temporary space where loving emotions could be expressed. From my father, I learned that alcohol could ignite emotions, while providing a temporary escape from the realities of life. From them both, I learned to normalize a life without deep intimacy and meaningful communication. From them both, I gathered information that I would eventually take into my future intimate relationships.

By most accounts, I've always been considered what you would call a *nice guy*. Though my mother and father had their shortcomings, they raised me to be a nice, respectful young man. And, for most of my life, I thought that being a *nice guy* was enough to make relationships succeed. It wasn't until I got into intimate relationships that my *nice guy* perception of myself was challenged. Truth is, I had absolutely no idea of *who or how to be* in relationships. I thought that the simple act of being present would always be enough. I simply could not understand why anybody would ask for anything more than that. I couldn't understand why intimate relationships would demand more than I was prepared to give. I figured that if I wasn't physically abusive or intentionally trying to hurt anybody, that should be sufficient. *I'm one of the good guys*, I thought. What more could I possibly give? If it was enough for my friends, I figured that the same should suffice for my mate. I was always good at maintaining friendships. But, for the life of me, I couldn't understand why the success in my platonic relationships didn't translate into successful romantic relationships. My logical conclusion was that I had been dating the wrong people. Something was wrong with *them* because it damn sure wasn't anything wrong with me.

The increased demands for intimacy in relationships caused me to put emotional distance between me and the one doing the demanding. I wholeheartedly believed that my mate's needs for deeper intimacy was a character flaw in them—a flaw that showed up as them being *needy*. The pressure to give *what I did not have* compelled me to develop the perception that someone was demanding me to be someone who I wasn't authentically. Ultimately, the pressure caused me to abandon many of my early relationships. It wasn't until much later in life that I realized that my actions were no less violent, in impact, than those who physically assault women. While I never entered relationships with the intent of causing pain, my tendency to withdraw my presence and emotions, point blame at my mate, sabotage and abandon relationships, was emotionally abusive and *violent*.

Unbeknownst to many who knew me, I was experiencing an extreme amount of pain. My male indoctrination, however, taught me to mask that pain. While it looked like I may have been walking, and sometimes running away from relationships unscathed, nothing could've been further from the truth. While I knew that I often caused confusion and pain due to my early departure from relationships, I never saw myself as the author of these tragic stories. For many years, I resisted the notion that I was the creator of a reality that had become all too familiar. I often engaged in destructive behaviors, including alcohol and drugs, to numb my feelings and get a temporary escape from the truth. Sure enough, every time I awakened from a drug-induced, drunken stupor, I was ready to saddle up and recreate another story in an effort to forget the last one. My guilt and shame caused me to turn my back on the pain, which I didn't want to see nor take responsibility for.

For much of my adult life, I was clueless when it came to acknowledging my feelings and navigating intimate relationships. This was not always the case. As a young boy, before male indoctrination took place, I was very sensitive—unafraid to cry and show my emotions. Somewhere, during my formative years—which for me, lasted well into my 30s—I learned how to harden my emotions and suppress my ability to feel. I'm sure that the process started long before I was conscious of the fact that I was absorbing messages about who I was supposed to be. It probably started when, as a little boy, I was told by my parents and adults, "Stop crying before I *really* give you something to cry about!" Not only did I stop crying, but I also learned that whatever I was initially crying about was insignificant. The process continued as I was socialized into *manhood* by my peers, my neighborhood and institutions such as church and school. My indoctrination was bolstered by my involvement with a college fraternity. There, I learned to perfect my indifference to pain and divorce myself from the feelings associated with it. The combination of all these experiences taught me to suppress everything that was considered *feminine* – feelings, sensitivity, tenderness, compassion. On the contrary, it taught me to accentuate everything that was considered *manly*—toughness, aggression, competition and the ability to endure as much pain as possible without complaining. The shame-hardening process, which the psychologist William Pollack refers to in his book, *Real Boys*, had taken full control of me. Being clueless of my authentic feelings ensured my indifference to the pain of others, particularly the women I was intimately involved with.

I've always been a *truth seeker*. For so long, much of the truth I sought was found in external sources, such as books on ancient wisdom, religion, philosophy, mysticism and self-help. All the intellect in the world could not spare me the pain that came with the ignorance of *self*. I had been running away from myself for years. I was unable to see myself as the root cause and creator of my reality. For much of my life, I navigated intimate relationships in a way that would minimize my capacity to show vulnerability. My attempts to avoid pain only caused more pain—to myself and to whomever got close to me.

Until recently, I was unable to see how my perceptions and ideas about manhood caused much of my internal conflict. My angst was exacerbated, if not caused by, the system of patriarchy that exists in our society. Patriarchy and toxic masculinity delayed my ability to see myself as a responsible party in my relationship woes. I was not aware of the privilege I was afforded simply because I am a male. If a relationship failed, I was free to jump into another relationship, without the danger of being seen as a slut or a hoe, particularly by other men. Toxic masculinity makes it so that's all that matters—how you're seen by your male counterparts. As a result, I was able to elevate my manhood status by the number of women I was associated with. One may think that the accolades I received from being a *real man* gave me a huge ego boost. Nothing could have been further from the truth. Every ending to a relationship caused an internal blow that made me feel like a failure. The resulting pain caused me to slowly slip into a darkness that I almost didn't return from. My only saving grace at the time was my desire to know *why I was the way I was*. If for no other reason than to initially save my own life, the truth seeker in me wanted to dig deep to discover the motives and perceptions that fueled my actions. I chose to surrender my life to something greater than myself and began my journey of self-discovery. A huge part of that self-discovery came as I embarked upon a study to see how patriarchy and toxic masculinity kept me, and most men, imprisoned. The subsequent chapters represent some of what I found—information that illumined my understanding of myself and set the stage for what now has become my life's work.

CHAPTER 2
THE CONFLICT

T HE WORLD IS full of conflict. And wherever there is conflict, opportunities for transformation exist. These opportunities, however,
must be preceded by an honest assessment of the underlying issues that
act as the source of the conflict. Whether the conflict is between compet-
ing political and religious ideologies, or racial, ethnic or gender identities—what often serves as the foundation of the conflict is a need for
power, control and certainty. Rather than seeing conflict as a normal part
of human relations, it is often viewed as an undesirable occurrence, characterized by the need to be *right*. In the absence of constructive ways to
deal with conflict, it becomes an adversarial event that can easily descend
into violence—whether that violence is physical, mental or psychological.
Those who are not interested in resolving conflict are often the ones who
benefit from it. The need to be right eclipses concern for the *other* as it
becomes easier for those who historically have a voice to abuse those who
don't. This ongoing process then develops into systems that are utilized
to uphold the status quo. By minimizing the humanity of the *other*, it becomes easier, in the mind of the abuser, to negate the needs of those he
sees as inferior.

Historically speaking, the violence perpetrated by those who create
systems of power is most often found in the form of discrimination, with
physical violence often being the result of that discrimination. By labeling
others as second-class citizens, discrimination is justified by the oppressor
and is accompanied by preconceived notions of superiority and inferiority, which are ultimately meant to divide the powerful from the powerless.
For example, the concept of race is used to conjure up differences between
people of different ethnicities and skin colors. These differences are then
used to indoctrinate the greater society into accepting ideas of superiority
and inferiority.

The same is done as it relates to religion. Religion can also be used as a means to label, separate and discriminate. History has shown that violence has often been the end result of religious differences. Today, our nation, our world, is reaping the consequences of the notions of religious certainty and domination. The seeds of religious separation were planted early in our human history, and the effects can still be felt today. The very act of separation can be one that breeds violence. Just as the separation of races leads to ideas of racial superiority, the separation of religions can lead to claims of religious certainty—one religion claiming to be the *true religion*, while the other is the *false religion*. One only needs to glance at history to realize that religion has significantly contributed to the bloodshed and terrorism throughout our world.

The same can be said for the effects of gender discrimination. By designating one gender as superior over the other, the stage is set for tensions to arise due to the physical and psychological separation of the sexes. Gender violence is the unfortunate consequence of this phenomenon. Specifically, the most devastating, yet largely unaddressed form of this, is violence toward women. The National Coalition Against Domestic Violence website reports the following facts:

- Every 9 seconds in the U.S. a woman is assaulted or beaten.[1]
- One in five women has been raped in their lifetime.[2]
- One in every three women will experience domestic violence in her lifetime.[3]
- An estimated 1.3 million women are victims of physical assault by an intimate partner each year.[4]

---

1. Ronet Bachman and Linda Saltzman, "Violence against Women: Estimates from the Redesigned Survey," *Bureau of Justice Statistics Report*, August 1995, http://www.bjs.gov/content/pub/pdf/FEMVIED.PDF.
2. Patricia Tjaden and Nancy Thoennes, "Prevalence, Incidence, and Consequences of Violence Against Women," *National Institute of Justice Centers for Disease Control and Prevention, Research in Brief*, November 1998, https://www.ncjrs.gov/pdffiles/172837.pdf.
3. Patricia Tjaden and Nancy Thoennes, *Extent, Nature and Consequences of Intimate Partner Violence: Findings for the National Violence Against Women Survey* (Washington, DC: National Institute of Justice and the Centers of Disease Control and Prevention, July 2000), https://www.ncjrs.gov/pdffiles1/nij/181867.pdf.
4. National Center for Injury Prevention and Control, *Costs of Intimate Partner Violence Against Women in the United States* (Atlanta, GA: Centers for Disease Control and Prevention, National Centers for Injury Prevention and Control, 2003), http://www.cdc.gov/violenceprevention/pdf/IPVBook-a.pdf.

- Approximately 85 percent of domestic violence victims are women.[5]

Frederick Douglass, when speaking on women's rights, said the following,

> *A woman should have every honorable motive exertion which is enjoyed by man, to the full extent of her capabilities and endowments. The case is too plain for argument. Nature has given woman the same powers, and subjected her to the same earth, breathes the same air, subsists on the same food, physical, moral, mental and spiritual. She has, therefore, an equal right with man, in all efforts to obtain and maintain a perfect existence.*[6]

The alarming nature of the above statistics is at direct odds with the sentiment expressed by Douglass. Contrary to Douglass' words, the statistics paint the picture that far too many women are *not* treated honorably and are *not* able to live the *perfect existence* that he speaks about. In fact, the statistics point to the fact that violence against women is an epidemic that threatens to destroy the foundations of this country—justice, equality, life, liberty and the pursuit of happiness. For a country that considers itself to be advanced, and uses family values as a measurement of morality, these numbers give rise to a much deeper issue when it comes to relations between men and women.

In an effort to reduce gender violence, we must first endeavor to uncover the root(s) of such violence. The prior statistics, while concerned with incidences of physical violence, fail to take into account the ways in which violence can be perpetrated psychologically, mentally and financially. In fact, these forms of violence can be a precursor to physical violence or can occur simultaneously. In order for healthy relationships to exist, violence must be eliminated and replaced with healthy ways to communicate and handle conflict. Relationships, by their very nature, consist

---

5. Callie Marie Rennison, "Intimate Partner Violence, 1993-2001," *Bureau of Justice Statistics Crime Data Brief*, February 2003, http://www.bjs.gov/content/pub/pdf/ipv01.pdf.

6. Jone Johnson Lewis, "Frederick Douglass Quotes on Women's Rights," *About.com*, http://womenshistory.about.com/od/quotes/a/douglass.htm (accessed April 24, 2016).

of conflict. It is only in the absence of constructive ways to deal with conflict that it sinks to levels of violence. The need to be right, or exert control over another, is counterproductive to healthy relationships. Unfortunately, all too often, this need can be a fatal blow to relationships—figuratively and literally.

The dissertation project completed for New York Theological Seminary proposed a *Conflict Transformation* approach to uncover ways in which violence is perpetrated toward women, discover ways in which to reduce that violence, and create processes that will contribute to long-term peace and increase gender justice. A transformational approach to this issue dictates that we not only *look* at the immediate issue of violence toward women, but we also *see* beyond the immediacy to uncover its root causes. When speaking of conflict, the renowned conflict transformation specialist, John Paul Lederach, advocates the need for us to look beyond the normal auspices of conflict resolution or management—for these approaches often provide short-term results.

"Resolution often focuses our attention on the presenting problems. Given its emphasis on immediate solutions, it tends to concentrate on the substance and content of the problem. This may explain why there has been such a predominance of literature on negotiation techniques within the field of conflict resolution—from popular airport bookstands to the halls of major research institutes. In short, resolution is content centered.

Transformation, on the other hand, includes the concern for content, but centers its attention on the context of relationship patterns. It sees conflict as embedded in the web and system of relational patterns."[7]

I analyzed the relational patterns of men and women within the context of religion—specifically Christianity. I also used the Bible as the text from which I drew examples of how women are viewed, as well as Scriptures that are used and interpreted in such a way to inform men how to treat women. Biblical interpretations have been used for centuries to indoctrinate the masses and violate those who weren't part of the dominant class. The manner in which women are portrayed in much of the Bible, and the way that religious men throughout the ages have espoused the inferiority of women, has significantly contributed to the abuse of women worldwide.

---

7. John Paul Lederach, *The Little Book of Conflict Transformation* (Intercourse, PA: Good Books, 2003), 1.

In his book, *A Call To Action: Women, Religion, Violence, and Power*, Jimmy Carter says,

> *"The truth is that male religious leaders have had—and still have—an option to interpret holy teachings either to exalt or subjugate women. They have, for their own selfish ends, overwhelmingly chosen the latter. Their continuing choice provides the foundation or justification for much of the pervasive persecution and abuse of women throughout the world."*[8]

The preceding quote invites us to consider that religion, and the varied ways in which sacred texts are interpreted, is a source of the conflict. Violence, then, is the destructive result of this conflict. And, in the absence of biblical interpretations in Christianity that are inclusive, violence will continue to flourish. Therefore, the thrust must be to reinterpret Scriptures in a manner that views men and women equally – both being original ideas in the mind of God.

A deeper source of the conflict resides in the fact that many of those who read Scriptures believe them to be the infallible Word of God. In other words, they believe in the authority of Scriptures exactly the way they were written and currently presented—no questions asked. So, before any reinterpretation can take place, we must explore, or at least be willing to admit, that some Scriptures either contain errors or are obsolete—only pertaining to the context and the times in which they were written. For many Christians, the thought of this shakes the very foundation of their belief. Those who interpret the Bible literally, and believe in its absolute infallibility, often quote the following Scripture taken from 2 Timothy 3:16 (KJV): *All scripture is given by inspiration of God, and is profitable for doctrine, for reproof, for correction, for instruction in righteousness.*

With this Scripture as a defense, Christians throughout the ages have justified their tendency to diminish, exclude and discriminate against others who believe differently. And more often than not, many pick and choose the Scriptures they want to use for their benefit, while totally ignoring Scriptures that totally contradict the Scriptures they so ardently

---

8. Jimmy Carter, "Losing My Religion for Equality," *The Age*, July 15, 2009, http://www.theage.com.au/federal-politics/losing-my-religion-for-equality-20090714-dkov.html.

adhere to daily. For these reasons, we find just as much, or more, conflict *within* the Christian community as we do between Christianity and other religions. The emergence of different denominations within the Christian community is a direct reflection of the varied reliance on particular Scriptures and their accompanying interpretations.

For example, Pentecostals strongly believe that speaking in tongues is the sole evidence of the indwelling of the Holy Spirit, and many will use the book of Acts to support their claim. In fact, I had a reformed Pentecostal tell me recently that if they encountered a Christian, particularly one who did not, or had not, spoken in tongues, they didn't consider him or her to be *saved*. As one who was raised Baptist, I was not taught that speaking in tongues was the *definitive evidence* of the Holy Spirit. I was taught, using the book of 1 Corinthians as a reference, that speaking in tongues was one gift of many; therefore, it's not the only evidence of being *saved*. I, as a Baptist, was instructed to believe that *love* was superior to the gift of tongues. Both of these denominations have used the interpretation of these Scriptures as part of their respective doctrines. Followers of these denominations, therefore, come to believe in the authority of that doctrine and become susceptible to the exclusivity that indoctrination brings.

The same has been done for another divisive issue in Christianity—whether women are equal to men in the eyes of God. Those who believe in the inferior status of women are not just Bible literalists, but they also choose select Scriptures that support their belief. While there are two separate creation stories in the book of Genesis, those wishing to justify male dominance often rely on the second account of creation found in Genesis 2:21-23, as opposed to the first account of creation, found in Genesis 1:26-27. The two accounts read as follows:

> *Then God said, "Let us make human beings in our image, to be like us. They will reign over the fish in the sea, the birds in the sky, the livestock, all the wild animals on the earth, and the small animals that scurry along the ground"*

> *So God created human beings in his own image. In the image of God he created them; male and female he created them.* (Genesis 1:26-27 NLV)

"So the Lord God caused the man to fall into a deep sleep. While the man slept, the Lord God took out one of the man's ribs and closed up the opening. Then the Lord God made a woman from the rib, and he brought her to the man.

"At last!" the man exclaimed.

"This one is bone from my bone, and flesh from my flesh! She shall be called 'woman,' because she was taken from 'man.'" (*Genesis 2:21-23 NLV*)

The belief, according to the second account, is that woman is taken from man. For some, that's an indication that men are superior to women.

Before delving into these anchor Scriptures, and other Scriptures like them, we must first acknowledge the conflicting nature of the Bible. While many Christians believe the Bible to be the complete and final Word of God, there are others who believe that the Scriptures are inconsistent and fallible. The conflict seems to arise from whether people believe that God stretched His hand down from the sky to pen the Bible himself, or whether the Bible was written through men who were inspired by God. If we choose to believe the latter, then we have to ask ourselves whether the men who penned the Bible were fallible men, just as they are today. If not fallible, then must we consider the context in which the Bible was written? In other words, inclusive in the Bible are notions of what men thought *about* God during the times in which it was written. This would suggest that some Scriptures are fluid and that our understanding of God is evolving in nature. The tension that exists between these two views must be addressed as we look to increase peace and reduce the violence that the attachment to these views brings. Hence, our need to be certain and attached to a particular perspective is also a source of the problem. If one stays committed to the belief that the Scriptures reveal an ultimate and unchanging truth, then women, as well as others, will continue to be seen as second-class citizens. This view will ensure that women continue to be oppressed, not only in religious circles, but in society in general.

The intersection of religion and violence against women has widespread ramifications that reach far beyond the physical. In his book *Religion and Violence*, Robert McAfee Brown states,

"However, it is the subtler forms of violence, in which overt physical assault may not be present, that do the deepest harm. It is frequently made clear to women in the business world that they are viewed either as playthings for men or as threats to presumed masculine superiority. Women are often the recipients of subtle and not so subtle messages that advancement—even retention of employment—depends on compliance with the sexual advances of their male superiors, or that their "worth" is viewed in terms of physical attractiveness rather than professional competence."[9]

To illustrate this point, a recent Think Progress article was entitled: "Most Women In Silicon Valley Report Being Sexually Harassed. Most Men Play Dumb."

"To get a better sense of sexism in tech, a Silicon Valley venture capital firm launched a survey on sexual harassment. The results: Nearly two-thirds of women in tech reported unwanted sexual advances—but their male counterparts were completely unaware.

According to the survey, 60 percent of women in tech reported unwanted sexual advances, and of those who did, 65 percent said those advances were repeated and came from a superior. More than 30 percent felt unsafe in their work environments, an issue that was fueled by insufficient recourse for women who did report sexual harassment."[10]

As I expand the definition of violence in a later chapter, my intent is to show that violence includes all actions that are harmful to another. These would include financial disparities, emotional abuse, silencing the voice of women, as well as excluding women from positions of leadership within the church.

Any study of violence toward women would not be complete without an analysis of male privilege. Patriarchal standards and ideas of masculin-

---

9. Robert McAfee Brown, *Religion and Violence*, 2nd ed. (Philadelphia: Westminster Press, 1987), xv.
10. Lauren C. Williams, "Women In Tech Report High Levels Of Harassment. Men Say They Had No Idea," *Think Progress*, January 12, 2016, http://thinkprogress.org/economy/2016/01/12/3738390/kleiner-perkins-harassment-study (accessed April 24, 2016).

ity are the foundation from which this violence and oppression is born. The privilege of setting the standards has historically ensured that power remains in the hands of those who create the standards. Therefore, power and privilege will always go hand-in-hand. In the case of religion, there can be nothing more powerful than having the privilege to create the image of a male deity—a deity who is said to be the author and finisher of the rules that *subjugate* women.

Images create perceptions. Whether presented consciously or unconsciously, images bring to mind all of the characteristics and traits that have historically been associated with them. When presented with an image of a God who has certain physical characteristics, those who don't share in those physical characteristics can feel negated and unworthy in the sight of *God*. This can affect how we perceive, live and relate to one another. In *Feminist Mysticism and Images of God*, Jennie S. Knight invites us to examine those images: "We live out the images that inform us. Images of the divine, other people, and one's self are profoundly interrelated within each person's imagination. They affect every relationship, including the divine. For this reason, it is crucial that we examine the images that shape our lives. In the Christian mystical tradition, the divine is described as a mystery greater than any image or name can contain. At the same time, human minds use images to relate to the divine."[11]

An examination of the images presented to us, along with the impact and perceptions that these images have produced, is crucial to transforming the relational patterns among people. This is no easy task, as it will cause people to question and redefine the identity that they've held on to for all of their lives. In the process, however, the opportunity to reimage the divine will encourage people to reimage themselves, thereby creating a society that minimizes separation and maximizes oneness—increasing peace while decreasing violence.

---

11. Jennie S. Knight, *Feminist Mysticism and Images of God: A Practical Theology* (St. Louis, MO: Chalice Press, 2011), 2.

CHAPTER 3
HOLY OPPRESSION

F OR MANY CHRISTIANS, the roots of feminine identity and gender roles continue to be defined by strict adherence to biblical Scriptures, particularly the Genesis account of the creation and the fall of man. Throughout the years, various interpretations have been espoused. Among the many varied accounts, two facts have seemed to remain constant within traditional Christian theology—woman is inferior to man, and woman is the temptress who was ultimately responsible for the fall of man. The progression of thought throughout the centuries has shown anything but progress. Early church fathers, theologians and reformers were not subtle in their comments about women:

Tertullian, "the father of Latin Christianity," said,

> *"In pain shall you bring forth children, woman, and you shall turn to your husband and he shall rule over you. And do you not know that you are Eve? God's sentence hangs still over all your sex and His punishment weighs down upon you. You are the devil's gateway; you are she who first violated the forbidden tree and broke the law of God. It was you who coaxed your way around him whom the devil had not the force to attack. With what ease you shattered that image of god: Man! Because of the death you merited, even the son of God had to die...Woman, you are the gate to hell."*[1]

Thirteenth century Dominican theologian, Saint Albertus Magnus, stated:

---

1. Bibles, Wheels, and Brains, "Anti-Woman Quotes by Church Fathers," http://www.biblewheel.com/forum/ showthread.php?3349-Anti-Woman-Quotes-by-Church-Fathers (accessed April 24, 2016).

> *"Woman is a misbegotten man and has a faulty and defective nature in comparison to his. Therefore, she is unsure in herself. What she cannot get, she seeks to obtain through lying and diabolical deceptions. And so, to put it briefly, one must be on one's guard with every woman, as if she were a poisonous snake and the horned devil...Thus in evil and perverse doings woman is cleverer, that is, slyer, than man. Her feelings drive woman toward every evil, just as reason impels man toward all good."[2]*

Additionally, the fourth century theologian, Saint Augustine, who was highly instrumental in shaping Western Christian thought, and is often referred to as one of the most important Catholic Church Fathers, said the following as it pertains to the woman and the image of God.

> *"Woman does not possess the image of God in herself but only when taken together with the male who is her head, so that the whole substance is one image. But when she is assigned the role as helpmate, a function that pertains to her alone, then she is not the image of God. But as far as the man is concerned, he is by himself alone the image of God just as fully and completely as when he and the women are joined together into one."[3]*

As far as a woman's worth is concerned, he proposed the following,

> *"What is the difference whether it is in a wife or a mother, it is still Eve the temptress that we must beware of in any women...I fail to see what use woman can be to a man, if one excludes the function of bearing children."[4]*

The beloved Protestant theologian and reformer, Martin Luther, furthered these ideas about a woman's worth when he added that, "The word and works of God is quite clear, that women were made either to be wives or prostitutes."[5] He went on to say that, "Men have broad and large chests.

---

2. Ibid.
3. Valerie Tarico, "Twenty Vile Quotes Against Women by Church Leaders from St. Augustine to Pat Robertson," https://valerietarico.com/2013/07/01/mysogynistquoteschurchfathers/ (accessed April 24, 2016).
4. Ibid.
5. Ibid.

And narrow hips, and more understanding than women, who have but small and narrow breasts, and broad hips, to the end they should remain at home, sit still, keep house, and bear and bring up children."[6]

Our more contemporary Christian brothers echo the same sentiment when referring to a woman's *place*. The Official Faith and Message Statement of the Southern Baptist Convention (SBC) in the summer of 1998 stated, "A wife is to submit graciously to the servant leadership of her husband, even as the church willingly submits to the headship of Christ."[7] In the effort to sound more inclusive, the convention's current statement on women reads, "While Scripture teaches that a woman's role is not identical to that of men in every respect, and that pastoral leadership is assigned to men, it also teaches that women are equal in value to men."[8] Additionally, conservative Christian leader and Southern Baptist, Pat Robertson, stated the following in 1992: "The feminist agenda is not about equal rights for women. It is about a socialist, anti-family political movement that encourages women to leave their husbands, kill their children, practice witchcraft, destroy capitalism and become lesbians."[9]

The startling reality is that, while these quotes span centuries, the continuum of thought is virtually unchanged. It is for this reason that former president Jimmy Carter and his wife, Rosalynn, decided to end their relationship with the Southern Baptist Convention, the denomination to which he had devoted seventy years of his life. The 2000 decision by the SBC to reemphasize its commitment to Bible verses that call for women to be silent in church, and forbids women to have authority over men at church or home, was particularly troubling to Carter and his wife. As a result of the convention's decisions, Southern Baptist women would no longer serve as deacons, pastors, chaplains in the armed forces, or in seminary classrooms where men were present. The Southern Baptist Convention is not alone as a denomination whose practices subjugate women. The majority, if not all, Christian governing bodies, have forbade female leadership in the past, and still wrestle with their positions as it relates to women's status within the church.

---

6. Ibid.
7. Ibid.
8. Southern Baptist Convention, "Position Statements: Women in Ministry," http://www.sbc.net/aboutus/positionstatements.asp.
9. Television evangelist Pat Robertson in a 1992 fundraising letter.

Moreover, the Bible reinforces the second-class status of women through the explicit nature of stories and the experiences of women between its covers. This is highly significant as we look at the relationship between religion and violence—specifically violence toward women. It would be difficult for even the casual reader to ignore the violent nature of the above comments. Likewise, it would also be hard to imagine that these early perceptions of women have not found a home in the minds and behaviors of men today. It is not just in the explicit words of early church fathers, alone, that do damage to women. It is also in the underlying fact that much of the Bible itself was penned by men who embraced the notion of women as inferior and as the property of men. It is helpful, at this point, to offer some thoughts and criticisms of the Bible—the book by which much of mainstream America embraces as *the* definitive guide for knowing God.

THE BIBLE

"The Bible is divinely inspired, yet humanly interpreted and therefore contains some of the Word of God—and some of the word of man about God. The Bible is a wonderful guide to familiarize us with some basic concepts of God. However, God is neither confined to nor defined by the Bible. The Bible is not to be worshipped as God, but to be revered as a guide." [10]

For those who take the Bible as the inerrant, infallible Word of God, the above quote, by Pastor D.E. Paulk, can be hard to swallow. Some would even consider it blasphemous. But if the religious roots of violence are to be uncovered, then we must look at the Bible as an instrument that has been used to justify that violence. Since many Christians believe the Bible to be the full, complete and the literal Word of God, then the first task is to analyze the Bible in that context. This is a necessary undertaking, as many mainstream Christians believe that everything that was written in the Bible, starting nearly 3500 years ago, is applicable and useful for instruction today. For many, the culture, context and authorship of particular Scriptures are irrelevant. When encouraged to look at Scriptures in critical ways, a typical Christian response would be, "God said it, I be-

---

10. D. E. Paulk, *The Holy Bible of Inclusion* (Atlanta, GA: Cathedral of the Holy Spirit, 2011), 26.

lieve it, and that settles it!" Cheryl B. Anderson in *Ancient Laws & Contemporary Controversies*, tells the story of a biblical exercise she conducted in a Bible study class with teenagers who were preparing to be high school seniors. The purpose of the exercise was to encourage them to look at Scriptures critically and to not be afraid to question what they were reading.

> *"We read the Ten Commandments, and I pointed out how slavery was condoned, and we read Judges 19, a particularly heinous story about the gang rape of a woman, and I showed them how one of the underlying messages of the text is that it is better for a woman to be raped than a man.*
>
> *For one female African American student in the class, the exercise was a total failure. At one point, she had had enough, and she blurted out, "This is the Word of God. If it says slavery is okay, slavery is okay. If it says rape is okay, rape is okay."*[11]

This response is disturbingly problematic for a number of reasons, notwithstanding the fact that she was a woman *and* an African American. Her commitment to her religious indoctrination and biblical supremacy obviously superseded her identity as an African American female. Her response was not just a personal sanction of slavery and rape, but it also revealed her lack of compassion for those who were enslaved and those who had been raped in the past. It is hard to imagine that her views of slavery and rape, as it existed in the Bible, would not taint her views about those same atrocities being committed today.

Those who see the Bible as a rigid set of standards, lacking the fluidity that accompanies changes in culture, context or experience, see themselves as being *keepers of the faith*. In doing so, they condemn and marginalize those who are desperately seeking the inclusive love of God. By adhering to the strict laws of centuries past, they become complicit in the oppression and violence perpetrated against those they deem to be outside the will of God, including women who overstep the boundaries created by their patriarchal understanding of God.

---

11. Cheryl B. Anderson, *Ancient Laws and Contemporary Controversies: The Need for Inclusive Biblical Interpretation* (Oxford: Oxford University Press, 2009), 3.

For instance, due to a denominational directive, and an attempt to strictly adhere to Scripture, a Baptist seminary released a female faculty member in 2007. The justification for this action was taken from the book of 1 Timothy 2:12 (KJV): *But I suffer not a woman to teach, nor usurp authority over the man, but to be in silence.* The fact that this faculty member was a graduate of the same seminary had no relevance in their decision, nor did the fact that she had excellent teaching evaluations up until the point of them firing her. And when the definition of violence is expanded to include emotional and financial harm, I conclude that the action taken by the seminary was nothing less than violent. That Scripture, along with others in the Bible, has been used to prevent women from being pastors and preachers in the pulpit. It has virtually stopped them from holding any leadership position within the church. One fundamentalist pastor went so far as to preach that women should not even say, "*Amen!*" in church because the word implies that they agree with what is being said. In doing so, in his opinion, they would be disobeying the directive to be *silent* in church. While this may be an extreme example of Bible literalism, it still gives credence to the notion that men – particularly those in the church – have a loud voice in creating the oppressive atmosphere that other men live by.

BIBLICAL VIOLENCE

> "*The Bible teaches that a father may sell his daughter for a slave, that he may sacrifice her purity to a mob, and that he may murder her, and still be a good father and a holy man. It teaches that a man may have any number of wives; that he may sell them, give them away, or swap them around, and still be a perfect gentleman, a good husband, a righteous man, and one of God's most intimate friends; and that is a pretty good position for a beginning.*"[12]

The Bible is a very inspirational text. This cannot be denied. However, the Bible contains an inordinate amount of violence. The God of the

---

12. AZ Quotes, "Helen H. Gardener Quotes," http://www.azquotes.com/author/54086-Helen_H_Gardener (accessed April 24, 2016).

Old Testament is often portrayed as being jealous, angry and vindictive. Throughout much of the Old Testament, God reveals His violent nature through acts of war, killings, requirement of human sacrifices, endorsement of rape and abuses of women and children. Consequently, when that particular image is presented as the nature of God, it's not surprising that many would see the subjugation of women as part of God's plan.

Most heartbreaking are the incidences of rape in the Bible. The heartbreak is magnified when we consider the similarity between those events and incidences of rape today. Many stories in the Bible give indication that the patriarchal culture sanctioned violence and/or rape. Take the stories of Susanna (Daniel 13); the Levite and the Concubine (Judges 19:11-30); the rape of Dinah (Genesis 34); the story of Joseph and Potiphar's wife, which suggests that a "false rape charge" is more common than actual rape; and the rape of Tamar (II Samuel 13), for example. In these stories, violence against women is trivialized or overlooked; thus, giving the message that violations of women are less important than the rights of men and intrigue between nations.[13] The story of Tamar vividly illustrates this point.

The rape of Tamar in the book of II Samuel vividly illustrates how women were used, abused and discarded by men who believed they had the God-given right to do so. In the book, *The Cry of Tamar: Violence against Women and the Church's Response,* Pamela Cooper-White recounts the rape of Tamar in "The Crime of Amnon," the book's prologue.

> *"David's son Absalom had a beautiful sister whose name was Tamar, and David's son Amnon fell in love with her. Amnon was so tormented that he made himself ill because of his sister Tamar, for she was a virgin, and it seemed impossible to Amnon to do anything to her. But Amnon had a friend whose name was Jonadab, the son of David's brother Shimeah, and Jonadab was a very crafty man. He said to him, "Oh son of the king, why are you so haggard morning after morning? Will you not tell me?" Amnon said to him, "I love Tamar, my brother Absalom's sister." Jonadab said to him, "Lie down on your bed, and pretend to be ill, and when your father comes to see you, say to him, "Let my*

---

13. James N. Poling, *The Abuse of Power: A Theological Problem* (Nashville, TN: Abingdon Press, 1991), 155-156.

sister Tamar come and give me something to eat, and prepare the food in my sight, that I may see it, and eat it from her hand." So Amnon lay down, and pretended to be ill, and when the king came to see him, Amnon said to the king, "Pray let my sister Tamar come and make a couple of cakes in my sight, so that I may eat from her hand."

"Then David sent home to Tamar, saying, "Go to your brother Amnon's house, and prepare food for him." So Tamar went to her brother Amnon's house, where he was lying down. She took dough, kneaded it, made cakes in his sight, and baked the cakes. Then she took the pan and set them out before him, but he refused to eat. Amnon said, "Send out everyone from me." So, everyone went out from him. Then Amnon said to Tamar, "Bring the food into the chamber, so that I may eat from your hand." So Tamar took the cakes she had made, and brought them into the chamber to Amnon, her brother. But when she brought them near him to eat, he took hold of her, and said to her, "Come, lie with me, my sister." She answered him, "No, my brother, do not force me, for such a thing is not done in Israel, do not do anything so vile! As for me, where could I carry my shame? And as for you, you would be as one of the scoundrels in Israel. Now therefore, I beg you, speak to the king, for he will not withhold me from you." But he would not listen to her, and being stronger than she, he forced her and lay with her."

"Then Amnon was seized with a very great loathing for her, indeed, his loathing was even greater than the lust he had felt for her. Amnon said, "Get out!" But she said to him, "No, my brother, for this wrong in sending me away is greater than the other you did to me." But he would not listen to her. He called the young man who served him and said, "Put this woman out of my presence, and bolt the door after her." (Now she was wearing a long robe with sleeves, for this is how the virgin daughters of the king were clothed in earlier times.) So his servant put her out, and bolted the door after her. But Tamar put ashes on her head, and tore the long robe she was wearing, she put her hand on her head, and went away, crying aloud as she went."

"Her brother Absalom said to her, "Has Amnon your brother been with you? Be quiet now, my sister, he is your brother, do not take this to heart." So Tamar remained, a desolate woman, in her brother Absalom's house. When King David heard of all these things, he became very angry, but he would not punish his son Amnon, because he loved him, for he was his firstborn."[14]

The story of Tamar overflows with episodes of violence perpetrated against her. The rape of Tamar is obviously the most heinous of the encounters she had to endure. The act itself is a violation of her humanity and a testament to the ugly truth that her body did not belong to her. Not only was the physical violation an indication of her not having bodily ownership, but the fact that Amnon and Jonadab conspired to bring the rape about points to the attitude men had about women in that day—that they were fair game to be manipulated for the pleasures of men. And while it may have been common to hear of incestuous relationships during those times, non-consensual sex should never become *common*, but rather seen as violent, in whichever circumstances it occurs. To add to the tragic event, this would serve as Tamar's initiation into the world of sex. To be sure, rape is no less tragic when it's perpetrated against women who are not virgins. But one can't help but to feel moved by Tamar's innocence, particularly in light of the full story.

The trauma that accompanies rape goes well beyond the physical violation alone. It alters one's psyche. The Power and Control Wheel, developed by the domestic abuse intervention programs, displays the variety of abusive behaviors and tactics that men use when perpetrating physical and sexual violence against women. The use of male privilege, coercion and threats, intimidation, isolation and emotional abuse, as well as minimizing and denying, are just some of the violent tactics that are used to maintain power and control. The story of Tamar, when seen in its totality, demonstrates that the physical violation was surrounded by much of what we see on the Power and Control Wheel. The fact that Tamar was at the beck and call of the men in her life gives us a clue of the expectations that were placed upon women, involuntarily. Tamar was expected to cook and follow any other directives from David or her brothers. Although accept-

---

14. Pamela Cooper-White, *The Cry of Tamar: Violence Against Women and the Church's Response*, 2nd ed. (Minneapolis: Fortress Press, 2012), 24.

ed at the time, the use of male privilege was, and still is, a form of violence. When men treat women as servants, make decisions for them, and take it upon themselves to define women's roles, they are engaging in psychological abuse.

Tamar was not only expected to cook and feed her brother, when requested, but she also did not have ownership over her own body. This was evident by the fact that, when begging her brother not to commit the vile act of rape, she told Amnon that she was sure that the king would give her to him if he was to only ask. In other words, regardless of how she felt about it, if he simply requested her sexually, then the request would have been granted.

After the act of rape, Amnon was overcome with such a feeling of disgust for her that he asked Tamar to get out. Despite Tamar's plea for him not to put her out—that doing so would be worse than the physical violation itself – Amnon did so anyway. Not only did he put her out, but he had the door bolted behind her. As Tamar went away, crying, we are confronted with the emotionally violent nature of Amnon's actions. The abandonment, humiliation, guilt and shame that Tamar is left alone to deal with only adds to the horror of the story. Additionally, Amnon's actions blatantly minimized the abuse that Tamar was facing, which added to her emotional stress. This can be seen by the fact that, long after the violation, Tamar remained a desolate woman. According to the patriarchal culture of the time, losing one's virginity, even by rape, diminished her value. She was permanently damaged, so much so that we never hear from Tamar after this incident. According to the standards of the time, she was useless.

Tamar's anguish was further exacerbated by the fact that her own father, King David, did nothing when he heard what had happened to her. As the story goes, King David became very angry, but he refused to punish his son because, as his firstborn, *he loved him*. I cannot imagine the emptiness, isolation and despair that Tamar must have felt. Not only was she a victim of incest and domestic violence, but the conspiracy of silence surrounding the event only heightens the depravity of her experience. And although some form of retribution took place, it must be noted that it didn't come until two years later. What happened of Tamar in the meantime?

In the end, we hear no more of Tamar in the Bible. The rest of the story, which began in 2 Samuel 13, continues for 19 more chapters and only focuses on the men in the story. We hear nothing of Tamar's feelings—we are only left to speculate. We hear no significant feelings of remorse for Tamar, although we do hear about King David's remorse when Amnon is killed by his brother two years later. Astonishingly, the story is more about the status and frailty of men's egos and relegates Tamar to a mere *collateral damage* status. The entire story of Tamar reeks with violations that mirror the abusive experiences of women today. As Pamela Cooper-White clearly and succinctly lists the abuses faced by Tamar, one cannot help but notice that her experience sounds eerily familiar to the experiences that victims of sexual violence experience today.

- Tamar was sexually assaulted, not by a stranger, but by someone she knew.
- The violation took place, not in a dark alley or in a desolate park, but by a member of her own family, at home.
- Tamar was exploited through one of her most vulnerable traits—her kindness and her upbringing to take care of the other.
- Tamar said, "No"; her "No" was not respected.
- When Tamar sought help, she was told to keep quiet.
- The process for achieving justice and restitution was taken out of her hands entirely and carried forward by her brother. It became men's business.
- In the end, it was her perpetrator for whom her father mourned, not for her.
- The end of Tamar's story happens without her.

Without the knowledge that the latter story is a biblical account of rape, one could very well believe that these events were the accounting of a rape that happened as recent as yesterday. Consider the story of Carole, a friend of mine whose story is similarly heinous and, unfortunately, not uncommon. For the purposes of the project, her name has been changed to protect her identity.

CAROLE'S STORY

Carole is a 53-year-old woman who was molested by her next door neighbor between the ages of 8 and 10 years old. In addition, her father was killed in a tragic accident when she was 13. As she grew into a young woman, she kept silent about the molestation and internalized the trauma of her early experiences. As it turns out, the first man that she ever dated beat her. It was at this point that Carole realized that the relationship was mirroring what she had seen with her mother and father. Being raised in the church, however, Carole resorted to *relying on her faith* and being the woman she believed God would have her to be.

Eventually, Carole met her brother-in-law's nephew, who was a junior deacon in the church. They would later get engaged. She truly believed that being with a man of God would be a redemptive act and that he, of all people, would be the one to treat her like a godly woman should be treated. After all, not only was he a deacon, but his uncle - her brother-in-law - was a minister. The titles alone were enough to garner her loyalty and trust. Unfortunately, not long after that, the relationship ended due to infidelities on his part. One day, while stopped at a traffic signal, she noticed that her ex-fiancé was in the car right next to her. He asked if he could see her; Carole agreed to meet him at a friend's apartment. She was excited about the possibility of reconciling the broken relationship. What followed was a brutal beating, accompanied by date rape, punctuated by the conception of a child. Again, Carole moved on with her life, all the while internalizing the trauma. As if a physical move would help relieve the pain, she moved to Atlanta.

Carole returned to the church and subsequently got married to a minister who was physically violent, as well. She eventually got divorced, but remained in the church. She began to notice that the men of the church, particularly the clergy, started treating her as if she was wearing a scarlet letter. Although the clergy knew about the domestic violence that had previously taken place, no one ever spoke about it. After the divorce, she asked the leadership of the church to bless her new home. To her horror, they showed up and commenced to perform some type of ritual in the home that mirrored an exorcism. The last straw came one Sunday during the church-wide prayer time. She was totally outdone as she watched her ex-husband, the abusive minister, approach the pulpit to offer prayer for the church. That was enough for Carole to finally leave the church. Her ex-husband eventually became pastor of that church.

Like Tamar, Carole would say that she became a *desolate woman* after this experience—even surviving a suicide attempt. The trauma caused her to swear off men, as she found it easier to develop intimate relationships with women. The devastating experience was further compounded by the fact that her family did not offer her the solace that she needed when she shared the experience with them. Her older sister, who was married to a minister, was too attached to her traditional role as a minister's wife to offer Carole the love and support that she needed. It took a long time, and lot of forgiveness, for Carole to embrace God's healing power.

The stories of Tamar and Carole, while centuries apart, speak to the universal pain associated with sexual violence, and to the attitudes of "godly" men who perpetrate, or are complicit, in these offenses. Remember, according to the Bible, King David, Tamar's father, was said to be "a man after God's own heart." This alone can paint the picture that God condones, or at least ignores, the rape of women. Tamar and Carole were both raped, shamed and discarded. Carole was left to her own devices in her attempt to find some semblance of peace and reconciliation within. Likewise, we never hear about Tamar again after the tragic incident. In both cases, the perpetrators never took an ounce of responsibility and never figured into the *justice equation* for either woman. When perpetrated by *lay* strangers, these experiences are traumatic enough. But the devastation is multiplied when the perpetration *and* the response from "godly men" supports and magnifies the environment in which the violence takes place.

THE SILENCE OF THE CHURCH

> *"At our best, we clergy think we are sensitive to the issue of domestic violence because we are sympathetic to victims. At our worst, we ourselves are perpetrators of violence through our preaching and our behavior."*
>
> *Rev. Joan Ishibashi, Minister in the United Church of Christ and Associate Conference Minister for Administration and Resources, Honolulu, Hawaii*[15]

For the most part, the church remains conspicuously silent on the issue of domestic violence, rape and sexual assault. Whether intended or unintended, silence is often synonymous with complicity. Unfortunately, for

---

15. Al Miles, *Domestic Violence: What Every Pastor Needs to Know* (Minneapolis: Fortress Press, 2000), 1.

many victims of these heinous crimes, the words of Dr. Martin Luther King, Jr. will remain, even after the healing process has been actively engaged and the perpetrator brought to justice. "In the end, we will remember not the words of our enemies, but the silence of our friends."[16]

In the earlier accounts of Tamar and Carole, not only did the perpetrator abandon the victims, but justice further eluded the women when the significant men in their lives were silent in response to their pain and trauma. In Tamar's case, King David refused to punish, or even acknowledge the crime of Amnon. In Carole's case, the clergy, as well as her family, gave no credence to her suffering. The responses should cause us to ponder two questions: 1) Why are godly men often unresponsive to violence against women? and 2) When they are responsive, how do those responses continue to perpetuate the culture and climate of violence?

Reverend Al Miles has been publishing articles and speaking about the role that pastors can play in preventing and eliminating domestic and family violence, since the 1990s. In his book, *Domestic Violence: What Every Pastor Needs To Know*, the introduction poses the question, "Where are all the pastors?" In it, he refers to his experiences conducting conferences for family and domestic violence. He noticed that it was a common occurrence for clergy, particularly male clergy, to be conspicuously absent when those subjects were addressed. Unfortunately, the lack of clergy involvement did not go unnoticed by the participants either. The following excerpt puts his feeling into words:

> *Embarrassed and often feeling defensive, I, too, was having a difficult time explaining or understanding the lack of pastoral involvement. Several times each year, the hospital at which I was then director of chaplaincy would host pastoral care conferences on a number of moral issues. The workshops least attended, by far, were the ones dealing with the problem of violence in the home. Further, even though many pastors invited me to speak at their churches on this subject, seldom would any of them attend the sessions. This was especially true of male pastors.*
>
> *Angered and frustrated by this lack of pastoral participation, I developed a policy: I'd speak on domestic or family violence issues*

---

16. Martin Luther King, Jr., "*Loving Your Enemies*," Sermon delivered at Dexter Avenue Baptist Church, Montgomery, Alabama, November 17, 1957.

only at those churches where the pastor themselves agreed to attend the workshops. I soon discovered that this course of action was also not foolproof. Many clergy members readily agreed to my stated condition of being present at the workshops. But, shortly after the sessions started, the pastors would mysteriously disappear and never return. When I began confronting clergy people about this behavior, they all offered the same justification: an unexpected emergency had arisen, I was told. Curiously, these "emergencies" rarely occurred when I spoke on other topics.

If the mere *presence* of a loving and supportive individual can make a difference for someone experiencing trauma, then I have to believe that the *absence* of supportive individuals can send a strong message, as well. The resistance of clergy members to gain information and receive training in the area of family and domestic violence can be interpreted as actions that condone the behaviors of perpetrators. Ironically, the condoning of the violent behaviors of men is nothing new, biblically speaking.

In addition to Tamar's experience in 2 Samuel 13, there are other instances in the Bible where women were not only raped, but that rape was condoned. And when interpreted by misogynistic men, one might assume that men's acceptance of rape is synonymous with God's intention. Following are a few scriptural references that give indications that rape was common and acceptable. Perhaps the attitudes of today's clergy remain rooted in the consciousness that produced these Scriptures.

If a man happens to meet a virgin who is not pledged to be married and rapes her and they are discovered, he shall pay the girl's father fifty shekels of silver. He must marry the girl, for he has violated her. He can never divorce her as long as he lives.

Deuteronomy 22:22-29

Watch, for the day of the Lord is coming when your possessions will be plundered right in front of you! I will gather all the nations to fight against Jerusalem. The city will be taken, the houses looted, and the women raped. Half the population will be taken into captivity, and the rest will be left among the ruins of the city.

Zechariah 14:1-2 NLV

"Here, take my virgin daughter and this man's concubine. I will bring them out to you, and you can abuse them and do whatever you like. But don't do such a shameful thing to this man." But they wouldn't listen to him. So the Levite took hold of his concubine and pushed her out the door. The men of the town abused her all night, taking turns raping her until morning. Finally, at dawn they let her go. At daybreak the woman returned to the house where her husband was staying. She collapsed at the door of the house and lay there until it was light.

Judges 19:24-26

While the actions indicated by the above Scriptures may be outdated in our society, the consciousness that underlies these actions cannot be as easily dismissed. While considering all the reasons why the clergy were noticeably absent from the conferences and presentations given by Reverend Al Miles, I had to consider that *godly* men, still rooted in religious traditionalism, had perceptions about women that were closely aligned with those who authored the preceding Scriptures. In a further attempt to understand the religious roots of violence toward women, I interviewed Pastor D.E. Paulk, a fifth-generation preacher and Senior Pastor of Spirit & Truth Sanctuary, a radically inclusive spiritual community in Decatur, GA. Spirit and Truth Sanctuary, unlike traditionally minded churches, is spiritually located within New Thought Christianity.[17] Pastor D.E, as he is affectionately known, has had a spiritual evolution that has spanned the gamut, from Pentecostal and charismatic preacher, to what some would call an interfaith heretic. What follows is an excerpt of that interview in a question and answer format.

ME

As one who's been in the church your entire life, how have you seen biblical language used to suppress others, particularly women in the church?

PASTOR D.E.

It's so prevalent that it's almost hidden because it becomes common

---

17. BeliefNet, "New Thought," http://www.beliefnet.com/Faiths/Christianity/
New-Thought/Index.aspx (accessed April 24, 2016).

culture. The common story is of Eve being the one that tempted her husband, and so the curse of man supposedly coming through Eve to the Old Testament stories determines what a woman's worth is. They actually give a figure of shekels and even say that a younger woman is worth more shekels than an older woman. You know, if you follow that on through, there's really only one book, well two, the book of Ruth and Esther, neither that were necessarily authored *by women*, but sort of *about women*. The scourge of Mary Magdalene never being accepted by the other apostles or disciples, yet being arguably the closest to Jesus. Peter refused her, the Council of Nicea refused her gospel. So it's, you know, part of a different set of gospels. It's been common language that bled into modern church culture where women from Paul's teaching were to be silent in church. At some point, they were allowed to sing in church, but could not teach. A woman should be silent in church. If she has a question, she should ask her husband at home, "For I will not suffer a woman to teach me," is Paul's doctrine. It turned into modern church culture, even when a woman was obviously anointed to teach or preach. They would never call them pastor or reverend or preacher. They would call them church mother, mother so-and-so, mother this, mother that. Finally, they would say prophetess a little bit, but the oppression has been so prevalent that it has almost gone unnoticed because it's just been such a part of our common culture, very familiar.

ME

Have you seen changes in the course of your ministry? If so, what changes have you seen as far as women's participation in church? Have you seen any changes in titles or their inclusion in this whole message?

PASTOR D.E.

Sure! There's been some significant strides. There are now, in some denominations, women who are the senior pastors of the church. There's a specific church that has a woman as their senior pastor, but the denomination said, "We won't recognize you as part of us if you don't take her out and put a man in." The local church said, "She is our pastor and you can take us out of the denomination if you must."

ME

This is recent?

PASTOR D.E.

This is in the past couple of years at a large church. There is still some waging of which consciousness we're going to fall into. But you see some uprising, even if it's in local churches saying we're not going to be bound by these ancient doctrines of men.

ME

Being familiar with the stories in the Bible about women being offered as the spoils of war, how would you say that these stories play into the consciousness of male leaders within the church today?

PASTOR D.E.

Well, not only from a biblical perspective, but just from a religious perspective in general. That plays into the treatment, the denigration of women and the abuse. It all goes back to the literal mind. Paul has a teaching in 1 Corinthians 3 that says, "The letter," and that word comes from the root "the literal." "The literal kills, but the spirit gives life." And whether it's Christianity, or it's Islamic, when radical groups take over an area, they see women as part of their prize. The women become sex slaves or whatever they want to use them for. But all that comes from literal interpretations of - not God's Word to man, but man's word about God - that we call either the Bible, the Quran or the Bhagavad Gita. They are man's attempts to understand God, but they come through a lot of culture and opinion. Even with some of the writing from 2000 or 3000 years ago, it's still that language and the ancient archaic culture that is still oppressive in the modern day. This is because of the literal minds that can't update their religion with the way that, not God is changing, but *man's ideas about God* are changing.

ME

What would you suggest for men who are in a church with literal biblical interpretations, looking to Scripture for their authority, but also being presented with the different way in which Jesus treated women?

PASTOR D.E.

Well, you see a little of a dichotomy with Jesus. Hebrews 5… "in the days of His flesh." When Jesus was still encumbered, a bit unconscious of the greater divinity that was about to shine through Him, there was still some culturalism, some tribalism that was happening, some chauvinism that was happening in there. He refers to His mother at some points as just "woman," you know. "Woman, I have nothing to do with you." That's not only His ego talking; some of that is His culture talking: "Why is this woman?" "Who is my mother?" "Who is my father?" There are also some moments where He is approached by women of other nations, other cultures, and He says to them, "A woman should not approach." But later, you see this evolution happening in Him where He is with the Samaritan woman at the well, at Jacob's well, and she tries to go back into that consciousness. "Jews just don't speak to Samaritans. Women don't speak to men." And He said, "The hour is coming when all those labels are about to fall off and we're going to be seen truly as a divine family." So as Jesus progressed in Hebrews 5, "having been perfected," He became the author of eternal salvation. We must be perfected–the men in churches, the men who are reading literally, the men who are trapped in culture as Jesus was, must graduate from that literalism into the Christ anointed, awakened mind that knows that the Bible is a guide to man, but that the Bible is not infallible. That's a big hurdle for many people. It was written by men, to men, and the Spirit of God does find its way into the pages. But we must rightly divide between what's opinion, what's culture, and what really is eternal truth. But there's a Scripture that says, *Be not conformed to this world, but be transformed by the renewing of the mind.* Men who are trapped in ancient, archaic teachings about women, and the keeping of a woman in her place, experience no transformation. Their minds are not being constantly renewed. That's what made Jesus special. He learned His culture, but He was constantly professing, *"Man shall not live by bread alone, but by every word that proceeds…"* There's a constant proceeding word that sometimes religion doesn't make space for.

ME

There are many women, as well, who are still under that same consciousness. They come up in church and believe that they have no place in leadership. What would you suggest for women who are trying to come out from under that yoke and pursue ministry now?

PASTOR D.E.

My exhortation would be just to think generationally. This is not really God's plan for your daughters, for your granddaughters. I don't know that I believe in generational curses, but sometimes there's a breaker of a cycle of consciousness. Whether that's being the first who graduates with a degree in your family, the first who starts their own business...there's many firsts in families. As a woman, even if it's the tradition or a vicious cycle in your family, there is enough strength within each of us to be the breaker of that cycle. And there's not going to be a lot of accolades or praise given to the breaker of it. The praise will come from the other generations that look back and say, "I, as a woman, would not have been a doctor. I would not have been a lawyer, a preacher, a pastor, a politician, an entrepreneur, a television mogul, had it not been for my mother, who showed me that I could be just as good as a man. I could be everything that God has called me to be."

The above interview does well in bringing attention to the consciousness that has historically undergirded the treatment of women in the Christian church. Just as thoughts become words, and words become actions, so it is that consciousness gives way to scriptural language that becomes embedded in the religious mind. In this case, language repeated throughout the centuries became *gospel* for many.

BIBLICAL LANGUAGE

Biblical language, including the reference to God as a *Father* and *He*, accounts for much of the justification men use to abuse women and children. While many men would deny this, it is helpful to revisit Robert McAfee Brown's words as he recounted the progression of his own understanding as it related to violence. He stated the following as he was preparing his second edition of *Religion and Violence.*

"There is one form of violence, however, to which I was oblivious during the original writing that now stares at me from the text and makes me both embarrassed and penitent. That is the degree of my employment of sexist language, which is an act of violence (in the basic meaning of a "violation of personhood") against women readers and, because of the false world it depicts, against men as well."[18]

The notion that God is *male* is just as disturbing and damaging as the notion that God is *white*. Language, as well as images, are adopted by those who relish power to exert control over their victims by aligning themselves with an authoritative God. James Newton Poling, in *The Abuse of Power: A Theological Problem*, states how this power can be used as justification for the abuse of women and children.

"For some victims, abusers used God to justify their behaviors. One perpetrator told his son that he was "beating the devil out of him," and said God would not accept a little boy who did not obey his father. Another perpetrator told his daughter that oral sex was her punishment for refusing to come in by curfew and that "by God, I am your father."

For others, abusers' allusions to God were indirect. Phrases such as, "I am your father. You should do it because I said so" or "This is something all fathers teach their children," implied that parental authority cannot be questioned. Since parents serve with god-like power in the lives of children, the implication, in the mind of a child, was that abuse was part of the order of things that included God.

In some cases, victims of abuse experienced confusion because the church made specific analogies between God and fathers when supporting parental authority. Polling also reports that many victims found it difficult to make a distinction between the abuse and their images of God. Consequently, you can imagine that any woman who has experienced sexual abuse at the hands of her father may have a hard time worshipping or submitting to *Father God*.

---

18. Robert McAfee Brown, *Religion and Violence*, 2nd ed. (Philadelphia: Westminster Press, 1987), viii.

Reverend Shaheerah Stephens, Pastor of Transforming Love Community, recalls her experience with her own father and the challenge to reconcile that image with the image of *Father God*. As a little girl, she remembers being taught that God was a male—to be referred to as *Father God*. The difficulty with the image arose from having a strained relationship with her father. Her father was not dependable and couldn't be trusted. Therefore, it was challenging to embrace the promises of a God who was deemed *Father*. She also saw God as someone to be feared and someone who would be quick to punish, mainly due to her father's effort to instill fear in his children. The physical attacks incurred by her mother at the hand of her father only served to crystallize the image of God as a violent presence to be feared, who was primed to punish at any given moment. It took years and the help of counseling for Reverend Shaheerah to awaken to the damaging perceptions created when God is seen solely as a *male* and as a *father*. She experienced her healing as she began to refer to and experience God as more than just a *father*. Initially, she began to refer to God as *Mother God* and/or *Mother-Father God*—a reference which was easier due to her loving relationship with her mother. Ultimately, she began to see God as a pure Spirit, a loving presence, which was neither male nor female. While some may have always seen God as genderless, her story, and similar stories from other women, give indication of how injurious the teaching of a gendered God can be.

The scope of the violence emanating from our images of God is widespread. Whether it's physical, emotional, psychological or economic, the violence perpetrated by religion can span centuries and do generational damage. The great thinker, religious teacher, anti-violence educator, Jiddu Krishnamurti[19] reminds us that violence has many faces and can take many forms. He also reminds us of the deep work that remains to be done to eliminate violence.

> *"Violence is not merely killing another. It is violence when we use a sharp word, when we make a gesture to brush away a person, when we obey because there is fear. So violence isn't merely organized butchery in the name of God, in the name of society or country. Violence is much more subtle, much deeper."*[20]

---

19. J. Krishnamurti, "An Overview of Krishnamurti's Life and Work," http://www.jkrishnamurti.org/about-krishnamurti/biography.php

20. Quotes Gram, "Jiddu Krishnamurti Quotes," http://quotesgram.com/ jiddu-krishnamurti-quotes (accessed April 24, 2016).

CHAPTER 4
THE PROBLEM WITH PATRIARCHY

Patriarchy is the single most life-threatening social disease
assaulting the male body and spirit in our nation.

—*bell hooks*

IT SHOULD COME as no surprise to discover that some men have no idea what the word *patriarchy* means. From a feminist perspective, men's ignorance of the word is confirmation of a society that is built on patriarchal values. Patriarchy can be defined as a "social system in which the role of the male as the primary authority figure is central to social organization, and where fathers hold authority over women, children and property. It implies the institutions of male rule and privilege, and is dependent on female subordination."[1] The fact that some men are unaware of the word, gives support to the notion that those who create and maintain a system that thrives off dominance do not have to concern themselves with the collateral impact of its existence, particularly when that system benefits them. Not all men, however, are intentional in patriarchy's application. It is important to remember that patriarchy is a system; therefore, the urge to indict all men in its prevalence would be misguided. It is not unreasonable to assume that many men unconsciously participate in this system, while simultaneously considering themselves to be fair and equitable human beings. Hence, that is the very nature of patriarchy—it is so heavily embedded into the fabric of our social order that males and females make conscious and unconscious decisions every day that support the oppressive values of patriarchy. These everyday practical decisions are often born out of the gender rules and roles that patriarchy demands.

---

1. http://www.princeton.edu/~achaney/tmve/wiki100k/docs/Patriarchy.html, s.v. "patriarchy."

I'm reminded of the story my mother-in-law once told me. She and her friend, who happened to live in the next door apartment, were planning to run a few errands. Before leaving, her friend made sure that she cooked dinner and left it on the stove for her husband. When they returned from their trip, her friend's husband was waiting at the front door to their apartment—upset because he had waited too long for his wife to get home to fix his plate. Rather than eat when he got hungry, he chose to wait with the expectation that his wife would fix his plate when she got home. The fact that she cooked for him at all, totally escaped him.

This occurrence, which was highly consistent with other evidence of patriarchal privilege in the relationship, is a stark example of not only how gender roles persist, but also how patriarchal expectations fail to consider the labor of women. Indeed, as creators of the rules in a patriarchal society, men retain the privilege of not having to be aware of the impact that privilege has on others.

In the above example, the husband had the privilege of not even being remotely aware of the patriarchal standards that are at work. As Allan G. Johnson points out in *The Gender Knot: Unraveling Our Patriarchal Legacy*,

> *"A key to maintaining male privilege is to devalue women by making them and what they do invisible. This happens, for example, when cleaning the house and taking care of children is viewed as nonwork or when a woman's ideas are ignored, only to be noticed and adopted when suggested by a man."*[2]

He assumed that taking care of his needs was categorized as *nonwork* for his wife, simply because that was what she was *supposed* to do as a wife. Meanwhile, he also maintained the assumption that for him to fix his own plate was *work*. Gendered expectations, within the family, are full of examples of how patriarchal standards govern the way in which men view the roles of a wife.

I'm told of another situation where a husband, who was accustomed to hanging out with the guys after work on Fridays, begrudgingly reported to his friends that he could not attend the after-work festivities because

---

2. Allan G. Johnson, *The Gender Knot: Unraveling Our Patriarchal Legacy*, 3rd ed. (Philadelphia: Temple University Press, 2014), 145.

he had to *babysit* his children at home. His wife, who usually assumed the responsibility of taking care of the kids, had a prior engagement that she had to attend. The reality of his admission impresses upon me the utter imbalance that patriarchy produces. The husband believed that for him to watch his own children was *babysitting*. The absurdity of the statement further underscores these concepts of *work/non-work* and *visibility/invisibility* in a patriarchal society. Unfortunately, women do not have the privilege of defining the rules or the boundaries. That right is reserved for men, as they have the advantage by operating in a system characterized by male dominance.

Male dominance ensures that men hold the positions of authority in political, economic, legal, religious, educational, military and domestic realms. Under a system of patriarchy, corporate CEOs, religious leaders, school principals, heads of state, and those who are considered heads of household, are all positions that are typically reserved for men. If a woman holds one of those positions, she is often considered an exception to the rule and her success continues to be measured by male standards. As Allan Johnson points out when speaking of these double standards, men rarely must face the same scrutiny.

> *"It is a test rarely applied to men ("I wonder if he'll be as good a president as a woman would be") except, perhaps, when men take on the devalued domestic and other caring work typically done by women, such as child care and housework or caring for an elderly parent. Even then, men's failure to measure up can be interpreted as a sign of superiority, a trained incapacity that actually protects their privileged status ("You change the diaper; I'm no good at that")."*[3]

This same standard is clearly evident in areas of income and wealth as the balance of power is always tipped in a man's favor. The very fact that the average man working full-time makes 30 percent more than the average woman gives a clear glimpse as to whose work is valued more. In spite of the fact that the majority of college graduates are women, they continue to lag behind men by occupying low-status, low-paid occupations. Even when women begin to occupy positions that are traditionally held

---

3. Ibid., 6.

by men, they still find themselves in lower-ranking and lower-paid positions. Simultaneously, men who occupy positions traditionally held by women, such as nursing and teaching, are still more highly paid than comparable women and are more likely to advance to leadership positions. The same disparities exist in politics, as women make up just 19 percent of the U.S. Congress, despite being over 50 percent of the population. In our universities, particularly in science, female students are seen as less competent than their male counterparts and are less likely to be offered jobs. And despite being the backbone of the modern church, women continue to suffer extreme amounts of oppression within the church. In fact, while many of the previously mentioned institutions continue to develop covert methods in which to discriminate against women, the church is an institution that engages in the overt oppression of women by denying them positions of power and leadership within its ranks.

BIBLICAL PATRIARCHY

Before delving into how patriarchy reveals itself within the Christian church, it is helpful to understand what *biblical patriarchy* is specifically. Vision Forum, an evangelical Christian organization, sets forth the following as the "Tenets of Biblical Patriarchy."

- God reveals Himself as masculine, not feminine.
- God ordained distinct gender roles for man and woman as part of the created order.
- A husband and father is the head of his household, a family leader, provider and protector.
- Male leadership in the home carries over into the church: only men are permitted to hold the ruling office in the church. A God-honoring society will likewise prefer male leadership in civil and other spheres.
- Since the woman was created as a helper to her husband, as bearer of children, and as a "keeper at home," the God-ordained and proper sphere of dominion for a wife is the household and that which is connected to the home.
- Christian parents must provide their children with a thorough Christian education, one that teaches the Bible and the biblical view of God and the world.

- Both sons and daughters are under the command of their fathers as long as they are under his roof or otherwise the recipients of his provision and protection.
- The age-integrated communities of family and church are the God-ordained institutions for training and socialization and as such provide the preferred pattern for social life and educational endeavors.[4]

With these tenets as a background, we can now look at the face of patriarchy within the church and the challenges it has presented for men and women alike. While this understanding of biblical patriarchy is promoted by an evangelical Christian organization, these tenets also bleed into other traditions of Christianity.

Nineteenth century author and political activist, Helen H. Gardener[5] once said,

> *"This religion and the Bible require of women everything, and give her nothing. They ask her support and her love, and repay her with contempt and oppression."*[6]

It is no coincidence that while women have long been the *backbone* of the church, they continue to be treated like a mere *rib* within the operation of that church. The reality of that truth brings into question the authority of the woman's creation story found in the book of Genesis 2: 21-23:

So the Lord God caused the man to fall into a deep sleep. While the man slept, the Lord God took out one of the man's ribs and closed up the opening. Then the Lord God made a woman from the rib, and he brought her to the man. "At last!" the man exclaimed. "This one is bone from my bone, and flesh from my flesh! She will be called 'woman' because she was taken from man."

Despite all of the advances that women have made in every arena of society, the church remains as a bastion of patriarchy. Patriarchy is so em-

---

4. Vision Forum Ministries, "The Tenets of Biblical Patriarchy," https://homeschoolersanonymous.files.wordpress.com/2014/04/the-tenets-of-biblical-patriarchy-vision-forum-ministries.pdf (accessed April 24, 2016).
5. Freedom From Religion Foundation, "Helen H. Gardener," https://ffrf.org/news/day/dayitems/item/14154-helen-h-gardener (accessed April 24, 2016).
6. AZ Quotes, "Helen H. Gardener Quotes."

bedded in its fabric that gender roles in many churches have remained consistent throughout the centuries. In recalling the roles of women in the church I grew up in, the role of Sunday School teacher sticks out. Women were permitted to teach and be the caretakers of children, but they were certainly not allowed to *preach to* or *pray for* the congregation.

In a male-dominated system, particularly the church, the privilege to interpret the rules—in this case, the Scriptures—rests with the pastor, bishop or other name given to the head of the church. And when the leader places himself as the interpreter of *God's Word*, most of the congregation just follows along like sheep, unaware of where they're being led. Even when one has the slightest intuition that something said does not sit well with his or her conscience, he or she resists the urge to speak out for fear of being called rebellious, or worse—*unsaved*. To think for oneself is certainly not encouraged in a system of conformity. As a result, well-meaning men, through their silence, become complicit in the oppression of women within the church. This is often the consequence when religious leaders portray themselves as the mouthpiece of God, and then interpret selective Scriptures to instill fear, compliance and guilt in the minds of congregants. And just as Eurocentric images and language were used to advance the cause of white supremacy, biblical images and language are used to perpetuate the patriarchal system in and beyond the walls of the church.

When interviewing Lori Robinson, rape survivor and author of *I Will Survive: The African-American Guide to Healing from Sexual Assault and Abuse,* I asked her to what extent she thought patriarchy contributed to an environment where sexual, physical and psychological violence takes place. She responded in the following manner.

I would say, contributes, is not even the word; it's the foundation of the environment that produces and perpetuates violence against women or gender-based violence of all types. So patriarchy, or a male-dominated society, by definition, it is a society in which women are less valued than men and which men give themselves. It's accepted society-wide that men are entitled to power and control over women. Then it's kind of just a rich breeding ground for the types of behavior...these types of behaviors.

RELIGIOUS ROOTS OF PATRIARCHY

Former bishop of the Episcopal Church, scholar and spokesperson, John Shelby Spong, invites us to uncover the roots of patriarchy.

> *"If an attitude finds expression in every prevailing religious system in the world, and in almost every society, one begins to suspect that this attitude has its roots in something very basic in our humanity. Religion incorporates and explains human content far more than it creates human content. Therefore, religion becomes the place where we begin to search for answers to the sin of patriarchy, and when we do so the sins of scripture in the form of the terrible texts about women in the Bible come into view."*[7]

Simply put, patriarchy is a violent system. When male privilege is used to treat a woman like a servant, define women's roles, or prevent women from making major decisions—a violent act has taken place. If this is so, then we must conclude that the Bible, through certain texts, encourages violence by teaching that a woman is from man and not from God, and therefore, not capable of being an independent being with independent thought. After all, 1 Corinthians 11:7-9 states specifically that: *for man is made in God's image and reflects God's glory. And woman reflects man's glory. For the first man didn't come from woman, but the first woman came from man. And man was not made for woman, but woman was made for man.*

Not only is the text violent, but the interpretation and application of the text is even more violent, particularly when that interpretation is done void of the cultural context in which it was written. Unfortunately, this is a practice that happens far too often—in the name of staying true to biblical Scripture. Pastor Steven L. Anderson, of Faithful Word Baptist Church, believes women should not say, "Amen!" in church. In essence, Pastor Anderson believes in staying true to the following Scriptures, that women must remain silent in church.

---

7. John Shelby Spong, *The Sins of Scripture: Exposing the Bible's Texts of Hate to Reveal the God of Love* (San Francisco: HarperSanFrancisco, 2005), 74.

Women should learn quietly and submissively. I do not let women teach men or have authority over them. Let them listen quietly. For God made Adam first, and afterward he made Eve (1 Timothy 2: 11-13 NLT).

Women should be silent during the church meetings. It is not proper for them to speak. They should be submissive, just as the law says. If they have any questions, they should ask their husbands at home, for it is improper for women to speak in church meetings (1 Corinthians 14: 34-35 NLT).

For literal Bible believing Christians, such as Pastor Anderson, the admonishment is clear—women have their place in the church and at home. The adherence to the aforementioned Scriptures clearly indicates that there is no escape for women. They are under a patriarchal covering at the church, subject to the teachings of the male pastor. They're under a patriarchal covering at home, subject to the teachings of their husbands. Many of the men, including pastors, who succumb to or perpetuate this teaching, would swear that they are not the intentional oppressors of women. Most would say that they are simply following the Scriptures and that they have no choice but to obey God. This is a scary thought, as it indicates the depth of patriarchy's effects in the religious mind. Truthfully, what men would call their obedience to the Scriptures is nothing more than their attempt to maintain power and control over women. It's not hard to do when men convince the masses that God is made in their image. And with that, long-standing, Bible-based gender roles have withstood the test of time—no more apparent than the role of *wife*.

THE NANCY MURPHY STORY

In the same way, you wives must accept the authority of your husbands. Then, even if some refuse to obey the Good News, your godly lives will speak to them without any words. They will be won over by observing your pure and reverent lives

1 Peter 3:1-2 NLT

In *The Resignation of Eve,* Jim Henderson tells us the story of Nancy Murphy, who is now the executive director of Northwest Family Life, an agency dedicated to helping the victims and perpetrators of domestic violence. Nancy grew up as the daughter of missionaries, so presenting the message of Jesus to the marginalized was nothing new for her. She grew up versed in the Christian way, and headed off for college. There, she involved herself in Christian activities, where she would meet the man who would eventually become her husband. He was passionate about Jesus and read his Bible with enthusiasm. She was so excited about starting a life with this saved, strong man of God, whom God had brought into her life. On the third day of the honeymoon, she woke up, after having a bad dream, and told her husband that she wanted to go outside and pray to release the feeling of the dream. It was at this point that her husband told her to stay in bed. While she was taken aback by his forceful tone, she went outside to pray anyway. As she was praying, her husband came up from behind and began hitting her and swearing at her. Needless to say, she was quite shocked. That was the first time that she had heard him speak like that or act like that. Her shock was intensified when he told her, "Your life is never going to be the same again." It was from this moment on that everything changed. As the violence escalated, Nancy searched for a way to cope, while attempting to keep her marriage intact. In his book, Jim Henderson recounts Nancy's experience and her thoughts as she weathered the violent storms.

Nancy, of course, had been trained in the evangelical way and understood what Scripture said about divorce. "The parts of the Scriptures I knew about wives and marriage read like this: 'Wives, likewise, be submissive to your own husbands, that even if some do not obey the word, they, without a word, may be won by the conduct of their wives, when they observe your chaste conduct' (1 Peter 3:1-2, NKJV). She pointed out to me that this passage was preceded by reminders from the apostle Peter about Jesus' willingness to suffer unto death.

> *"I mentally recounted my wedding vows," Nancy continued. "What had I committed to? 'I take you to be my lawful wedded husband, for richer, for poorer, in sickness and in health 'til death parts us.'"*

> *"Well, I wasn't dead, so it sounded as if it was my job to adjust my behavior to 'win' my husband. This type of behavior was all new to me. I was totally unaware that violence could exist in a marriage where both were Christians."*

"I didn't have more than two or three minutes before the violence escalated, and I had to make a quick choice. I had just married a man I loved. It was just the two of us...alone, finally. We'd already made love. I felt as if I had no other choice. I turned to him and said, 'I'm sorry.' I told him I wouldn't 'disobey' him again, and I begged him to calm down. He did. He explained that I had done something that had caused him to hit me. I'd left the room when he'd told me not to. I promised never to do it again, and I felt a big piece of my heart shrivel to the size of a dried pea. It had been so large just the day before. That was over now."[8]

Nancy spent the next 10 years trying to win her husband over—so he could stop hitting her. On a few occasions, she even turned to others for help. One night, while staying at the home of their pastor and wife, Nancy's husband left the house and didn't return until the early morning hours. He told Nancy that he had picked up a hitchhiker and had sex with the woman because Nancy didn't have time to talk to *him* anymore. When she told her pastor's wife about the abuse, the first lady suggested that perhaps it was happening because the two of them weren't attending church faithfully. In the meantime, while talking to the pastor's wife, the pastor and Nancy's husband went out to talk. Upon return, the pastor acknowledged to Nancy that he knew her husband had treated her badly. However, he said, after spending the whole day with him, he concluded that he was a special guy and offered him the assistant pastor position, after the two of them worked their problems out.

> *"You have to learn to get up from the table when love is no longer being served."*
>
> *—Nina Simone*

Nancy finally found the courage to leave after she witnessed her husband kick their youngest child. That was the wake-up call she needed. With the help of a friend, Nancy moved out and began a new journey. But not before an attempted reconciliation with her husband—advice that she got

---

8. Jim Henderson, *The Resignation of Eve: What If Adam's Rib Is No Longer Willing to Be the Church's Backbone?* (Carol Stream, IL: BarnaBooks, 2012), 50-51.

from another pastor. After her husband hit her again, she was intent on leaving for good. Through a network of friends, and Christians who were followers of Jesus, she found her way to Seattle, where her new life would finally begin.

Nancy's story is a prime example of how detrimental Christian patriarchy can be. At the expense of her own life, Nancy was completely convinced that her suffering was mandated by God in the name of being a good Christian wife. It took years of abuse, and the possible sacrifice of a child, for her to realize that only a God created and made in the image of patriarchal men would require such a sacrifice. Likewise, patriarchy, on its way to oppressing women, oppresses the minds of men, as well. The patriarchal mindset of the church often relieves men of their own senses. As a result, many men blindly follow the instruction of their pastors and, without original intention, oppress their wives, mates and other women in the church, all in the name of God. This, of course, is another privilege of patriarchy—the privilege to be unaware of the overt and collateral damage that maleness provides.

Jim Henderson's *The Resignation of Eve* also invites us to see how patriarchy can encourage women to be complicit in their own oppression—though these women would prefer the term *obedience* than *oppression*. Henderson also tells of a woman, who, in obedience to her Christian faith, believes wholeheartedly that women are unequipped to lead. Staying true to Scripture, she believes that a woman's submission, and her adherence to specific gender roles, is the recipe for a happy marriage. Simply put, her philosophy is that men would feel more affirmed and take more authority if women learned how to be quiet and submit to their leadership. While many traditional Christian women see this as a proven technique to keep the peace within a marriage, the cost of such peace can be contradictory to the self-worth and authentic voice of women. When I think about the power that patriarchal images of God wield, I am reminded of the difficult endeavor that women have in re-imaging the divine. Reverend Shaheerah's attempt to image God as feminine, mirrors the experience of many women who struggled to do the same. Jennie S. Knight, in *Feminist Mysticism and Images of God: A Practical Theology,* offers a glimpse of why this is so:

"My research with women in the Christian feminist spirituality movement revealed a complex of tensions they experienced when they challenged the "official" male God of their childhoods, trying to image the divine as feminine. For example, they realized that they did not consider women worthy to be representative of the divine because they did not experience women as powerful. Even though they had all been trying to change their image of the divine to a feminine image for a number of years, they still struggled to do so because they did not feel themselves, their mothers, or other women to be powerful or worthy enough to represent the divine. Their image of God had been largely created out of personality aspects of their fathers or of other men because they had difficulty seeing their mothers or other women as representative of the divine.[9]

This is the power of Christian patriarchy with its associated images. The tendency to diminish *self,* constitutes self-inflicted violence. The inability of women to see themselves as equal and intentional beings in God's creation reduces their agency in the world. A deep re-imaging of the divine must be undertaken if patriarchy is to be dismantled in the mind. God must be envisioned through a different lens if justice is to ever be a reality for women around the world. Until that day, ego-driven men will continue to make manifest the words of Nawal El Saadawi:

> *"Patriarchy needs god to justify injustice."*[10]

---

9. Jennie S. Knight, *Feminist Mysticism and Images of God: A Practical Theology* (St. Louis, MO: Chalice Press, 2011), 25.
10. Karen Tate, *Voices of the Sacred Feminine* (Alresford, UK: John Hunt Publishing, 2014), 1.

CHAPTER 5
THE MASCULINITY MYTH

*It is true that masses of men have not begun to look at the ways
that patriarchy keeps them from knowing themselves, from being
in touch with their feelings, from loving. To know love, men must
be able to choose life over death. They must be willing to change.*[1]

—bell hooks

A NY DISCUSSION OF violence toward women must, at its core, address the culture and the climate that engenders such violence. Inci-
dents of violence toward women do not exist in a vacuum. They occur
within the context of a society where violence is the norm. As it pertains
to violence, sociologist Orlando Patterson gives this critique of the violent history of our nation.

> *"America has always been a violent place. And quite apart from
> their involvement with slavery, Euro-Americans have always
> exhibited a perverse fascination with violence. The violence of
> Euro-American men against other Euro-American men, and
> against Euro-American women, needs no documentation. The
> law of the jungle, of an eye for an eye, has played and continues to
> play, a central role in the culture...Euro-American men exhibit a
> higher rate of homicide and other forms of violence than do the
> men of any other advanced industrial society...America is the
> only advanced industrial society that practices capital
> punishment...The experience, and fear, of violence among
> Euro-Americans is hardly new...The quintessential American
> myth is that of the cowboy...Central to that myth are the role of*

---

1. bell hooks, *The Will To Change: Men, Masculinity, And Love* (New York: Washington
Square Press, 2004), xvii.

violence and the reverence for the gun...Thus violence is not only
shunned and dreaded in American culture; it is also embraced
and romanticized."[2]

Psychologist Michele Toomey adds, "The pressures to speak and act violently are everywhere...Violence is not a deviant act; it is a conforming one."[3] And it has long been the case that boys and men are conforming at alarming rates. When looking at the gender disparities that exist when analyzing the perpetrators of violent acts, it leads one to believe that it is something about the ways boys and men are socialized that make them more prone to violence. Further analysis points to prevailing ideas of masculinity and the ways in which males are indoctrinated into that system.

While there is a growing concern about the need to address violence in our streets and homes, there has not been a widespread or sweeping analysis of that which reinforces violent, reckless, self-destructive behavior in men and boys, and what can be done to change it. And despite the continued proliferation of systems that thrive on male dominance and hypermasculinity, I am amazed at the failure of society to draw a definitive correlation between the way in which boys are raised and the violence perpetrated by the males. Perhaps it is the privilege afforded to those in power that allows them to ignore their own responsibility in the creation of violent societies. Myriam Miedzian, author of *Boys Will Be Boys*, blames the "masculine mystique" for creating a culture of violence among men, while also creating an environment in which men are afraid to oppose this system, publicly or privately. As a result, many of the men who have never even committed a significant act of violence become silently complicit in the maintenance of a culture dominated by oppressive and violent men.

Men are not born violent; rather they are born and socialized into a system that serves as an incubator for violence. According to Michael Kimmel, "The belief that violence is manly, is not carried on any chromosome, not soldered into the wiring of the right or left hemisphere, not juiced by testosterone. Boys learn it."[4] As one who continually strives

---

2. Orlando Patterson, *Rituals of Blood: Consequences of Slavery in Two American Centuries* (Washington, DC: Civitas/CounterPoint, 1998), 242-243.

3. Michele Toomey, "The Price of Masculinity Based on Violence," *Education Digest*, 58, no. 4 (1992): 44-46.

4. Michael Kimmel, "Searching for a New Boyhood: The Testosterone vs. Feminism Debate," *Voice Male: The Magazine of the Men's Resource Center of Western Massachusetts* (Winter 2000): 8-10.

to grow spiritually, mentally and psychologically, I maintain that what is *learned* can be *unlearned*. I wholeheartedly share in the belief that Jackson Katz states in *The Macho Paradox*:

> *"Since domestic and sexual violence are largely learned behaviors, it is important to reach boys before they learn to abuse girls. And since these types of violence are so closely linked to men's beliefs about what it means to be a man, it is also important to provide boys with alternative ideas about manhood to counterbalance all of the hypermasculine posturing and misogyny they encounter in their peer culture and the media."[5]*

As a boy, I can recall many of the messages that I received about being a "big boy." These ideas were undoubtedly the ideas I was to embrace as I became a man. I can remember statements such as, "Stop crying...big boys don't cry!" "Suck it up!" "Stop whining!" In my young mind, many of these messages translated into, "Don't show emotion and never let anyone know how you really feel." As a result, I learned at an early age to betray myself by denying the inner urges and yearnings of my spirit...particularly if those urges were inconsistent with the ideas of manhood that were being thrust upon me. To do so would have been detrimental to my male identity, resulting in an immediate dismissal from the boys' club. From that point on, I learned how to put limits on the expression of my feelings, thereby limiting my future ability to love. Little did I know that I was sacrificing my ability to feel so that I could take my place in a world where I would be considered a real *man's man*. Hindsight now reveals to me that by shutting down my ability to feel, I was also shutting down my capacity for intimacy.

Consequently, the first relationship that was characterized by a total lack of intimacy was the relationship with myself. This is the case for many men. The suppression of feelings and thoughts is directed inward, as men feel that they are not allowed to give outward expression to anything of a feeling nature...except rage of course. And this rage is often a byproduct of the anger that results from trying so desperately to live according to the patriarchal script – a script that is so embedded that many

---

5. Jackson Katz, *The Macho Paradox: Why Some Men Hurt Women and How All Men Can Help* (Naperville, IL: Sourcebooks, 2006), 228.

men are not aware of its impact until demands for intimacy are put upon them. The impact of this socialization cannot be understated.

The iconic bell hooks states, "Patriarchy is the single most life-threatening social disease assaulting the male body and spirit in our nation."[6] This assault finds its beginnings in the lives of our boys, with an even more devastating impact upon black boys. She goes further to say, "Oftentimes the patriarchal socialization that insists boys should not express emotions or have emotional caretaking, is most viciously and ruthlessly implicated in the early childhood socialization of black boys. The image of emasculated and castrated black males is so embedded in the cultural imagination that many black parents feel it is crucial to train boys to be "tough."[7] This point is well-illustrated as Houston A. Baker, Jr., in his autobiographical essay, "On the Distinction of 'Jr.,'" describes the psychological terrorism that takes place as black boys are socialized into patriarchal thinking:

> *"I am 11 years old, giddy with the joy of fire and awed by the seemingly invulnerability of my father. He is removing dead coals from the glowing bed of the furnace. He is risking the peril of flames. We are sharing...we are together...For some reason I am prompted to move with the pure spirit of being. I begin dancing around the furnace with light abandon. My voice slides up the scale to a high falsetto. I am possessed by some primitive god of fire. I feel joyful and secure. I am supremely happy, high-voiced, fluid. Then I am suddenly flattened against a limestone wall, bolts of lightning and bright stars flashing in my head. I have been hard and viciously slapped in the mouth as a thunderous voice shouts..."Stop acting like a sissy."[8]*

The above story is a common occurrence in many households in which boys grow up. It is yet another message that signals to boys that the free expression of feelings and creativity is not an acceptable representation of manhood. Unfortunately, many boys, in the attempt to garner acceptance and male closeness, accept this message and continue to acquiesce to these

---

6. hooks, *The Will To Change*, 17.
7. bell hooks, *We Real Cool: Black Men and Masculinity* (New York: Routledge, 2004), 86.
8. Ibid., 86-87.

notions of manhood throughout their lifetime. All the while, these men are unaware of the dangers that are to come due to the repression of their true feelings. Meanwhile, boys who reject these hardened notions of manhood, and dare to step outside of the box, are often ridiculed and subjected to brutality for not living up to patriarchal standards. Many of our boys are subjected to this trauma for fear that they may become "too soft." bell hooks refers to the term, *soul murder*, coined by the psychoanalyst Leonard Shengold, when describing this process.

Soul murder is the psychological term that best describes this crushing of the male spirit in boyhood.[9] Diminished self-esteem, low self-worth and chronic depression are often the results of what Alice Miller calls this "soul murdering" process. According to educator John Bradshaw, this depression is a consequence of their "true and authentic selves being shamed through abandonment in childhood."[10] Many boys, including myself, were shamed into accepting rigid notions of patriarchal boyhood. My own story comes to mind as I recall my tendency, as a little boy, to cry when my feelings were hurt by my father. I clearly remember being reprimanded and shamed for expressing my feelings in that manner. After all, *big boys didn't cry*. As a result, I eventually learned how to deny my feelings. Years of conditioning eventually translated into the abandonment of my true self. The inner conflict that ensued lasted well into my adult years and continues to be a focal point of my healing.

The conflict and inner tension that men experience can be directly attributed to the mixed messages they receive about manhood. On one hand, males are socialized to believe that their maleness reserves for them the right to be dominant, controlling and preferred—descriptors that many men use to bolster their sense of self. On the other hand, males are shamed, humiliated and ostracized when they display behavior that is not consistent with the rigid requirements of patriarchal manhood. The phenomenon, which most often has its genesis within the home of most boys, is heavily reinforced in the peer group. It eventually finds its way into all spaces where men gather...most notably, the sports and military culture, fraternities and gang culture. The pressure to maintain allegiance to patriarchal expectations can be psychologically devastating to the man who feels the unction to step outside the confines of those expectations. These

---

9. Ibid., 87.
10. John Bradshaw, *Healing the Shame That Binds You* (Deerfield Beach, FL: Health Communications, 2005), 65.

stories are played out in the private lives of men and the public places in which they gather, whether it's the locker rooms, boardrooms or the battlefield. Men cannot escape the pressures of patriarchy. Popular media, music and movies also reinforce the power of patriarchal indoctrination.

In the popular 1999 movie, *Analyze That*, Robert DeNiro is cast as mob boss, Paul Vitti. At some point in the movie, Vitti suffers a panic attack and tells his bodyguard that he needs to see a psychiatrist, but it has to be kept a secret. When Vitti finally meets Dr. Ben Sobel, played by Billy Crystal, he claims that *his friend* needs therapy. Dr. Sobel, recognizing that Vitti is talking about himself, suggests that his panic attacks, as well as anger issues, are most likely related to stress—a suggestion that Vitti vehemently denies. As the story progresses, Dr. Sobel uncovers that Paul Vitti's issues are due to unresolved feelings about his relationship with his father, as well as the unresolved grief associated with the blame he assumes for his father's murder, which he witnessed as a child. While the intention of the movie is to give a comedic edge to an otherwise cold-blooded mobster, it succeeds in sending the resounding message that men are not to express feelings—and to do so is to show weakness. Paul Vitti's insistence that his relationship with the psychiatrist be kept secret directly translates into his fear of being seen as someone who has feelings—an admittance that could be life threatening in the world in which he lives and operates. Similarly, many men in the real world experience significant amounts of trepidation when faced with the possibility of showing weakness or disloyalty to patriarchal norms; to do so is synonymous to the death of their manhood.

The dilemma that men face daily can develop into internalized rage or violence when healthy outlets for expressing feelings are not present. Donald Dutton, author of *The Batterer*, believes that the way out of this dilemma rests in providing men with the proper channels to acknowledge and feel pain. When speaking of black men, he states, "They must, like all wounded males, mourn the loss of what was never attained and attempt to integrate the good and bad aspects of what is still possible."[11] In the absence of proper channels, "trapped feelings of powerlessness" can engender rage. Violence toward self and others is often the alternative for the misplaced emotions that men internalize. The hatred, shame and confu-

---

11. Donald G. Dutton and Susan K. Golant, *The Batterer: A Psychological Profile* (Princeton, NJ: Recording for the Blind & Dyslexic, 2004).

sion that confounds these men is, most often, directed inwardly before outer manifestations appear. A man who has directed his anger at others has first directed it at *himself.* The outward display of his rage is but a symptom of his inability to express himself, as well as a consequence of the debilitating methods he uses to suppress his emotions.

Such was the case with many of the participants from The TLC, the group of men that I met with from Transforming Love Community. Calvin, one of the more vocal participants, acknowledged that it was his insistence on maintaining the "masculine mystique" that gave him need to express his dominance at home. This overwhelming need was born out of the fact that he really felt *powerless.* The conflict within led him to alcohol and drugs as a way to ease the pain and tension that he felt. Without realizing the source of the tension, he continued to numb himself with intoxicants, which in turn, increased his anger and frustration. During the workshop, he began to have glimpses of truth, realizing that he, and not just his wife at the time, had a significant responsibility in the demise of the relationship, as well as his estrangement from his wife. Up until that point, he had been blaming his wife for his troubles. In *We Real Cool: Black Men and Masculinity*, bell hooks references this tendency. "Scapegoating is a diversionary tactic. It allows the scapegoater to avoid the issues they must confront if they are to assume responsibility for their lives."[12]

Tom, another eager participant, expressed his frustration with being seen merely as a provider during his marriage. He recalled how when he attempted to express himself, he was seen as being weak. He, too, turned to drugs and alcohol to deal with his feelings of hurt and anger. I challenged Tom to consider whether he was upset with his former wife because she saw him merely as a provider, or if he was mad at himself for presenting himself as a provider at the outset of the relationship. My question was aimed at getting Tom to see that the ideas of masculinity into which he was indoctrinated only defined him as a responsible man if he kept a job, protected and provided for the material well-being of his family. When Tom temporarily lost the income, he had been accustomed to, he subsequently felt less than a man. Unfortunately, when he attempted to express how he felt to his wife, he was met with the same resistance from his wife. She, being indoctrinated by the same beliefs, saw Tom as

---

12. hooks, *We Real Cool*, 85.

less than a *real man*. It is not unreasonable to assume that outward displays of violence would follow, as both of these men began to direct their frustrations inward. As it is often said, *hurt people hurt people*. Michael Kimmel reminds us that the real enemy is not the person to whom this outward anger is directed. He states,

> *"Our enemy is an ideology of masculinity that we inherited from our fathers, and their fathers before them, an ideology that promises unparalleled acquisition coupled with tragically impoverished emotional intelligence. We have accepted an ideology of masculinity that leaves us feeling empty and alone when we do it right, and even worse when we felt we're doing it wrong. Worst of all, though, is when we feel we've done it right and still do not get the rewards to which we believe we are entitled. Then we have to blame somebody. Somebody else."*[13]

The more I continued to interact with these men, as well as analyze my own ideas of masculinity, I realized that most men, as a result of these trumped up ideas of masculinity, suffer from intense shame. This toxic shame is rooted in the false persona that men must display in order to not be seen as weak. Further shame is also brought on by the guilt associated with the outward displays of rage and violence that result from misplaced blame. John Bradshaw, author of *Healing The Shame That Binds You*, says, "Toxic shame is unbearable and always necessitates a cover-up, a false self. Since one feels his true self is defective and flawed, one needs a false self that is not defective and flawed." [14] He goes on to suggest that, "Toxic shame is the greatest form of learned domestic violence there is. It destroys human life."[15]

I'm reminded of when I was in my mid-twenties, suffering from the same type of identity complex. The prevailing ideas of masculinity encouraged me to *look the part* of a man before I really knew what a man was. It wasn't long before I was walking down the aisle, pretending to be someone I had never intimately known. I was making the commitment to be a husband – not because I wanted to—but because I wanted to

---

13. Michael S. Kimmel, *Angry White Men: American Masculinity at the End of an Era* (New York: Nation Books, 2013), 1.
14. Bradshaw, *Healing the Shame*, xvii.
15. Ibid.

look like a man who could commit. In other words, I was more concerned about how I looked to a woman than how I looked to myself. I was making what was supposed to be a life-long commitment, and I had no idea that I was supposed to *feel* some sort of way about that. My dad, society, religion, as well as institutional life had impressed upon me that life was about meeting obligations. If these obligations defined what a man was, I was willing to oblige. My indoctrination had taught me that I didn't have a choice. Little did I know, at the time, that I was committing *soul murder*. The betrayal of my *authentic self* would soon lead to the betrayal of the marriage. The death of *self* led to the death of the marriage.

This is the story of countless men who suffer alienation from their authentic selves. The impact to themselves, their children and women is of biblical proportions. To the modern-day Christian, the toxic shame produced also has biblical roots. The Bible story concerning the *fall of man* is one in which we become intimately familiar with Adam's shame due to his disobedience in the garden. According to the story, Adam was at first *naked and not ashamed*. In the attempt to become something that he wasn't created to be, Adam betrayed God by eating the fruit of the Tree of the Knowledge of Good and Evil. When God returned, he found that Adam was hiding himself. When God asked Adam why he was hiding, Adam responded by saying, "I heard you in the garden, and I was afraid because I was naked; so I hid." God's response, "Who told you that you were naked?" shows us how alternative messages we receive from others can often contradict who we really are. When Adam and Eve chose to become something other than what they were, they became naked and ashamed.

While the story is symbolic of mankind's condition, it is poignantly the case for the masses of men. Men, as the recipients of messages that encourage them to display hyper-masculine behavior, face an intense amount of shaming when they display any behavior that is inconsistent with the masculine façade. Consequently, when men suppress behaviors that have been labeled feminine, such as compassion, love and the outward expression of emotions, they are, in essence, betraying themselves. Scripture, when interpreted inclusively, provides us a basis for understanding the nature of mankind as including both the masculine and feminine aspects of creation. Genesis 1:26-27 reads,

Then God said, "Let us make man in *our* image, in our likeness, and let *them* rule over the fish of the sea and the birds of the air, over the livestock, over all the earth, and over all the creatures that move along the ground...So God created man in his own image, in the image of God created him; *male and female he created them.*"

With the understanding that the words *man* and *him* denote *mankind* in the above Scripture, attention must also be given to the use of the words *our* and *them*. Their usage begs the question, "Who is *our* and *them* referring to?" The end of the Scripture confirms that God created *him...male and female.* This leads one to believe that there is a dual nature to God's creation. If God created *them male* and *female*, then this would surely suggest that there is equal billing to the male and female aspect of God. This further suggests that there is a feminine nature encompassed in the divine, the presence of which contradicts the notion that God is solely male or masculine in nature.

The implication of this notion should be translated into our lived experiences. If we assume that, according to the above Scripture, that the male and female aspect of creation is an original idea in the mind of God, then we also must assume that females do not occupy a secondary status in God's kingdom. Further, the Scripture may also suggest that there is a male and female aspect to mankind...that mankind is incomplete without a symbiosis of the two. Therefore, to deny, suppress, or oppress an aspect of this creation is to deny what makes us fully human. However, if one maintains that Genesis 2:21-23 is the only authentic account of woman's creation, a different conclusion will be drawn. Genesis 2:22 reads,

> *So the Lord God caused the man to fall into a deep sleep; and*
> *while he was sleeping, he took one of the man's ribs and closed up*
> *the place with flesh. Then the Lord God made a woman from the*
> *rib he had taken out of the man, and he brought her to the man.*
> *The man said, "This is now bone of my bones and flesh off my*
> *flesh; she shall be called woman; for she was taken out of man."*

One can see how interpretation of the latter Scripture can lead to the belief that females were a secondary notion in God's creation rather than an original idea. These Scriptures, by themselves, can set the foundation for embedded beliefs about God's intention as it relates to gender, as well as the male/female identity and the associated gender roles. A more in-depth exploration of the religious and biblical contributions to gender identity will be discussed in another chapter. However, it remains important to note how ideas of masculinity are gleaned from Scripture.

The traditional ways in which boys and men are indoctrinated into masculinity demands that they suppress any thoughts and behaviors that can be interpreted as feminine. The documentary, "The Mask You Live In" by Jennifer Soebel, explores the indoctrination that boys receive from an early age by being told to, "Man up!" "Man up" means to essentially suck up your feelings and refrain from displaying anything that is contrary to being hard, aggressive and unemotional. The trailer to the documentary suggests that boys are falling into depression at alarming rates due to the pressure "to be a man." In essence, boys are being asked to hype up the masculine behaviors, while simultaneously suppressing the behaviors that we call feminine. Without the knowledge that they were created with the capacity to feel and express a wide range of emotions – and without the recognition that they have the inherent permission to display such emotions—boys and men suppress that which makes them a healthy, whole human being.

At some point during the second workshop with the Men of TLC in Detroit, I asked the men to list all of the behaviors that they associated with being a man. I then asked them to list the behaviors they deemed as being feminine. True to form, when listing masculine and feminine behaviors, men created a list that mirrored the indoctrination they received at a young age. The compiled list was as follows:

MASCULINE AND FEMININE BEHAVIORS

Masculine	*Feminine*
Strong	Crying
Leader	Maternal
Athleticism	Weak
Role model	Emotional
Dominance	Sensitive
Suppress feelings	Timid
Emotionless	Nurture
Tough	Teacher
Womanizer	Soft
Don't be a pussy	Friendly
Bravery	
Controlling	
Head of household	
Provider	

After the list was compiled, men saw a visual representation of the standards in which they had been desperately trying to live up to. One participant, Darryl, acknowledged that the masculine characteristics were given to him at an early age. He admitted that these descriptors encouraged him to live in a box—a masculine box – a box that he allowed to define him for the majority of his life. The significance of this was not lost on Darryl, nor was it lost on many of the other men. Darryl's story included time that he had done in the penitentiary. In recalling his story, I remember Darryl telling me about how his arrest had come to pass. As a young man in his early twenties, he was hanging out with a bunch of guys his age, when someone decided that stealing a car would be a "fun" thing to do. Darryl, not wanting to spoil the fun, and certainly not wanting to be a punk, went along with the program. When the guys finally got pulled over by the police, they were all arrested. Darryl chose to forego his opportunity to lessen his jail time, in favor of not being seen as a snitch. In the end, Darryl spent 13 years in the penitentiary because he chose to live up to a code that his indoctrination convinced him was manly. During the workshop, he anxiously shared his experience with these codes of masculinity, as he had long recognized that they were the culprit for the early decisions he had made in his life. Darryl's story is the story of a countless men who have fallen prey to the *masculine mystique.*

While it took jail time for a stolen car for Darryl to begin the process of awakening to the dangers of male indoctrination, the consequences are more severe for many other men. The confusion and frustration that comes from trying to live up to a false identity often engenders violence and abuse toward self and others. And, all too often, this violence has deadly consequences. Spiritually speaking, when searching for the roots of masculinity, it remains to me that masculinity is born out of patriarchy, and they both are born out of a god complex that men glean from the Bible.

THE BIBLE AND IMAGES OF MASCULINITY

Ideas of masculinity cannot be divorced from the patriarchal images that men have been bombarded with since they first stepped foot in a church. You and I may be hard pressed to find a church solely dedicated to Christian values, that doesn't teach men that they should be dominant leaders in their home and beyond. In fact, the men who are not *having the last word* in their homes are often considered to be weak and henpecked. Consider the following Scripture, which, while rarely preached openly in the church, encompasses the mindset of many men as they judge *manliness* in themselves or other men.

> *If a man's testicles are crushed or his penis is cut off, he may not be admitted to the assembly of the Lord.*
>
> *Deuteronomy 23:1 NLV*

With that Scripture in mind, it is not surprising that the phrases, "get some balls" and "she's got you by the balls," refers to the times when men are not expressing dominance as men, or when women have usurped their authority. In the effort to *grow some balls,* it wouldn't be uncommon for a man to leave church or a men's study group, and go directly home to reassert their authority. During The 700 Club's *"Bring It On"* segment, Christian fundamentalist Pat Robertson sought to advise a man who sent in a question about how to approach marital problems with his wife. Robertson remarked that, "He can't let her get away with this stuff," also noting that, although we don't *"condone wife-beating these days,"* perhaps the man could move to Saudi Arabia where a man could beat his wife.

While this may sound like an extreme evangelical response that many liberal Christians wouldn't buy into, I am reminded of the advice I got years ago from friends when I was experiencing some issues with my, then, wife. One friend was a Christian, who was extremely active in his Baptist church. The other did not regularly attend church, but had a Christian background. When I revealed to them some things that my wife had said to me, both of them responded by telling me that I should've slapped her. From their perspectives, a violent physical response on my part would've put things in their proper place. The response from Pat Robertson, as well as the advice from my friends, germinates from a place that endorses violence as a means of taking and keeping control. Hence, relationships that exist on a *dominant-subordinate* basis often use intimidation to preserve the form of the relationship. Intimate relationships founded on this principle are by their very nature—violent.

Biblical manhood cannot be separated from the messages that boys and men hear every day about *how to be a man*. Pastor, coach and former NFL player, Joe Ehrmann, shared the following words in a TEDx presentation designed to transform the culture of men and violence.

> *"The three most destructive words that every man receives when he's a boy is when he's told to be a man."*[16]

In giving a visual representation of the cycle that relates harmful ideas of manhood to violence, Pastor Joe identifies *socialization* and *social mandates* as starting points to developing the unhealthy habits that eventually lead to violence. It is my position that religion contributes significantly to the culture of socialization that boys and men receive. As he pinpoints *sexual conquests* as one of the myths of masculinity, I'm reminded of the conversations of my younger years when we men would attempt to justify sexual conquests by suggesting that if it was acceptable to God for biblical men to have multiple wives and concubines—then it should be acceptable for men today. Further, the Bible reveals that those sexual conquests are often accompanied by violence and perpetuated through rape. This

---

16. Joe Ehrmann, "Be A Man," Tedx Talks, February 20, 2013, https://youtu.be/jVI1Xutc_Ws (accessed April 24, 2016).

further cements the notion of women as the property of men, solely at the will of men's pleasures—an idea which lives well in the minds of men today.

As the best man in a close friend's wedding in the late '80s, I recall my friend discussing the changes that would take place in his sexual relationship with his wife now that he was married. His claim was that his wife was going to *give it to him* anytime he wanted because she was now his wife. When that didn't work out quite as planned, he found someone else to *give it to him* anytime he wanted—while he was still married, I might add.

While observing a court-mandated session for men accused of domestic violence, I witnessed the angst of a man who was put off by being required to attend. When given the chance to express his feelings, he blurted out, as if he had been holding it in for too long, "The Bible says she's mine and I can do whatever I want!" Apparently, he had resorted to violence when his sexual demands weren't met.

In her book, *The Second Sex*, Simone de Beauvoir said, "*In a society shaped by men, women are seen as relative beings existing only in relationship to men.*"

In order to reshape society, patriarchy and hyper-masculinity must be challenged by feminism. At its core, a reimaging of the divine must include a healthy balance of the *masculine* and *feminine*—a concept that I'll explore in the next chapter. Until this happens, patriarchal men will continue to shape *God* and the *world* in their image.

CHAPTER 6
CHANGING THE NARRATIVE
THE CASE FOR INCLUSION

T HE FRAMEWORK SURROUNDING the dissertation's methodology was grounded in Narrative Mediation. This framework offered the perfect opportunity for the participants to become increasingly aware of the social, cultural and religious contexts that have conspired to shape their perceptions and their conflicts. As the researcher, my task was to get men to realize how their perceptions of God, gender and manhood have contributed to the lived out narratives of their lives. Narrative Mediation was best suited to reveal to these men that conflict is often the result of outside stimuli, not some innate deficiency on their part. As men were able tell their stories, and hear the stories of others, they were more amenable to see these stories in the context of conflicting messages that they've received all of their lives. Narrative Mediation also allowed me to assist the men to externalize their conflict in such a way that they could see the imposition, and the damage, that external messages have had on them. It was then that men could be about the business of deconstructing dominant narratives, make discursive shifts, and begin the process of re-storying for the purpose of creating new narratives in their lives. It was the goal of this project for men to see how the social, cultural and religious narratives contribute to violence by promoting unhealthy perceptions of women. Then, invite them to embrace narratives that are non-violent and inclusive in nature—narratives created *by* them rather than imposed *on* them.

To shed light on how religious narratives inform our lives, we looked at the creation story found in the Bible. For many in the Christian tradition, this is a foundational story that sets the stage for further narratives that we adopt during our lives. It is also one of the stories most frequently referred to when defining the role of gender in God's kingdom:

Then God said, "Let us make man in our image, in our likeness, and let them rule over the fish of the sea and the birds of the air, over the livestock, over all the earth, and over all the creatures that move along the ground." So God created man in his own image, in the image of God he created him; male and female he created them.

Genesis 1:26-27 NIV

Then God said, "Let us make human beings in our image, to be like us. They will reign over the fish in the sea, the birds in the sky, the livestock, all the wild animals on the earth, and the small animals that scurry along the ground." So God created human beings in his own image. In the image of God he created them.

Genesis 1:26-27 NLT

At first glance, the two Scriptures above look identical. A closer examination reveals that they are not the same. The first Scripture is taken from the New International Version (NIV) of the Bible, while the second Scripture is taken from the New Living Translation (NLT) of the Bible. If I've learned anything from this project, it's that language is very important to creating perceptions. In mainstream Christianity, the above Scripture is considered to be one of those foundational Scriptures—the one that explains, particularly to new Christians, how *man* came into being. Notice that I used the word *man* in the previous sentence. There's another Scripture found in the book of Genesis that is historically used to explain how *woman* came into being.

Before we look at that Scripture, allow me to point out the differences with the two Scriptures above. In the very first line of the NIV version, we read that God said, "Let us make *man* in our image..." In the NLT version, we read that God said, "Let us make *human beings* in our image..." Some Christians may consider this difference to be minute and trivial. I don't. The use of one term or the other can have huge implications, particularly for someone who is not familiar with the Bible and is encouraged to interpret the Bible literally. Such a person is also apt to rely on the teachings and interpretation of a pastor, minister, Sunday School teacher, or anyone they deem more versed in the Bible. Such a person, who may want to have a patriarchal advantage, will likely focus on the term '*man*' while never stopping to consider, or even offer an explanation as to why, in the same sentence the term '*us*' appears before the term '*man*.' Who is '*us*'?

To further make my point about the usage of language, consider the implications of the phrase, "Let us make *human beings...*" The phrase is inclusive in nature and produces a totally different image in the mind of the novice reader. Later in my Christian development, I was encouraged to interpret *man* to mean *mankind* in that Scripture. However, this was only after I began to question the literalism of the Bible. Wouldn't it be interpreted easier if the writer just included the term 'mankind' from the very beginning? After all, the NLT version of the Bible was published only 20 years ago. Likewise, versions of the Bible that were intended to offer clarity by the use of modern language are a fairly recent phenomenon. The Living Bible, which is the predecessor to the NLT version, was published 45 years ago, in 1971. Both versions are considered babies when considering the life span of the Bible. The King James Version, which was the Bible that many Christians were first introduced to, was formally authorized in the year 1611 and was considered the standard for English speaking Protestants. The NIV version of the Bible, which the first Genesis Scripture is taken from above, is strikingly similar in language to the King James Version.

There are a few other terms and *pronouns* used in the Genesis Scriptures that should give the critical reader pause, or at least make one think about the language used. The terms *our* and *them* are collective pronouns that imply *more than one*. But the most obvious indication of gender inclusion in this creation story is in the last line of the Scripture that reads, "*...in the image of God he created him; male and female, he created them.*" By the way, that Scripture in the King James Version of the Bible reads virtually the same way. When interpreting that Scripture, one can assume either that God created *man* with male and female qualities, or God literally created males *and* females respectively, while the term "him" denotes *mankind*. Many of these theological questions can proceed from the specific version of the Bible that one reads, or the version that one is taught from—in which case, the interpretation is given by someone else.

In the desire to locate inclusive language in the Bible—or to even question why such language is elusive—two questions must be considered. Who did the writing, and who's doing the interpreting? Based on these questions, I've drawn significant conclusions and implications for future work based on my project. Of the 40 men who participated in the survey, 37 of them responded when asked which version of the Bible that they were raised on. Thirty-three of them cited the King James Version as the Bible of their early Christian experience. Close to 80 percent of them said that they were taught to interpret that Bible literally. The combination of these facts indicates that many men may still have a narrow interpretation of Scripture. However, this offers tremendous opportunities for transformation through the usage of inclusive biblical language.

Eric H. F. Law, an ordained Episcopal priest and multicultural consultant, recalls in his book, *Inclusion: Making Room for Grace*, the first time he discovered images of God as a mother. It was during the '70s while attending a Bible study group in college. This occurrence was very significant for him.

> *"The inclusion of the mother image of God allowed me to include the feminine side of myself as part of what God has given me. It allowed me to accept that side of myself that society considered feminine and, to my mind then, not godly. It allowed me to see and perceive the role of women with new eyes. It allowed me to appreciate and support the women's movement of the church. As my boundary was extended to include a different image of God, I became more open to meeting, listening, and learning from others who had a different perception and experience."[1]*

Law's experience was not unlike my own when I began to embrace and use language inclusive of a *mother* God. To give gender balance to my reference, I used the term *Father-Mother* God. As a man indoctrinated by patriarchy and masculinity, I did not find it difficult to change my terminology for God—which makes me question the extent of my indoctrination. But many of my male friends *did* have a problem with referring to God as anything other than *Father*. I knew men and women who shunned those who used the term *mother* when referring to God. And, like Eric Law, I found that the change in reference started me on a path to self-love, embracing my whole self, which included traits that I had formerly resisted because of the *feminine* stigma attached to them. My assumption

---

1. Eric H. F. Law, *Inclusion: Making Room for Grace* (St. Louis, MO: Chalice Press, 2000), 72-73.

is that many men resist referring to God as *mother* for the same reason, notwithstanding the fact that they had always been taught that God is *Father God* – and Father God alone. Perhaps the deep desire to be a *man's man,* and be likened to the image of their own fathers, contributes to their resistance of imagining God having to do with anything feminine. And perhaps my loving and respectful relationship with my own mother contributed to the ease in which I referred to God as mother. Nevertheless, the reference to God as Mother, or other feminine identities, is not new, though some may think it's a New Age phenomenon.

There is evidence that many ancient civilizations embraced divine feminine language and imagery, including Goddess worship. April D. DeConick, in her book, *Holy Misogyny,* points to the early Syrian Church that retained traditions about the Mother Spirit. Due to the retention of the Syriac dialect in some of the Aramaic Christian traditions, the memory of the female spirit was retained in the culture.

> *"As in Aramaic, the word ruha or "spirit" in Syriac is feminine.*
> *Even as late as the fourth century, well-respected Syrian*
> *theologians and poets such as Ephrem, Marcarius, and Aphraates*
> *still standardly conceive of the Holy Spirit as female."*[2]

Merlin Stone, in *When God Was A Woman,* reminds us of the women warriors and the matriarchal nations of Ethiopia and Libya that existed before the birth of Christ. In part of Libya, where the Goddess Neith was highly esteemed, accounts of the Amazon women still lingered in Roman times.[3] The warrior women of Libya did indeed revere the Goddess as their major deity and created sanctuaries for Her worship. Stone also reminds us that the concept of the Goddess was vital to Egypt.

> *"In prehistoric Egypt, the Goddess held supremacy in Upper*
> *Egypt (the south) as Nekhebt, symbolized as a vulture. The*
> *people of Lower Egypt, which includes the northern delta region,*
> *worshipped their supreme Goddess as a cobra, using the name Ua*
> *Zit (Great Serpent). From about 3000 BC onward the Goddess,*

---

2. April D. De Conick, *Holy Misogyny: Why the Sex and Gender Conflicts in the Early Church Still Matter* (London: Bloomsbury Academic, 2013), 21.

3. Merlin Stone, *When God Was a Woman* (New York: Harcourt Brace Jovanovich, 1978), 34.

known as Nut, Net or Nit, probably derived from Nekhebt, was
said to have existed when nothing else had yet been created. She
then created all that had come into being. According to Egyptian
mythology, it was She who first placed Ra, the sun god, in the sky.
Other texts of Egypt tell of the Goddess as Hathor in this role of
creator of existence, explaining that She took the form of a serpent
at that time."[4]

Indeed, the presence of a female deity, complete with language and imagery, is nothing new. At some point in history, this phenomenon was usurped, suppressed and replaced with the imagery of a male deity who created the universe and produced man in his own image, and created the female as an afterthought to be obedient to the man. Much of biblical Scripture that supports this notion has survived the centuries and still to this day is embedded in the minds of men.

At this point in time, however, I do not suggest that we continue to wage a war of extremes. It's past time to continue imaging God as solely male or solely female. A divine balance is necessary that recognizes the legitimacy of the masculine and feminine nature of the Divine. The only way to do that is to restore that which has been lost or suppressed. We must recognize this as the first step of restoring women to proper standing. The need for inclusive biblical interpretation has never been more vital. In the effort, we must also begin to highlight those biblical Scriptures that already produce images of equity and inclusivity. Moreover, we must shine a light on the words and deeds of the One who came to tear down the walls of division, destroy old labels and traditions, and recognize the full presence of God in women.

INCLUSION IN THE BIBLE

While there are Scriptures in the Bible that expressly support inclusion, of utmost importance is for the Bible to be read, taught and embraced with an inclusive spirit. Without an inclusive spirit, these Scriptures will be merely words on a page. Inclusive Scriptures are not new to the Bible—they've always been there. The fact is that more Scriptures have been interpreted through the lens of fear than they have through the lens

---

4. Ibid.

of an inclusive love. To make the point of the presence of inclusion in the Scriptures, consider Galatians 3:28.

> *There is neither Jew nor Greek, there is neither bond nor free, there is neither male nor female: for ye are all one in Christ.*

The above Scripture is taken from the King James Version of the Bible. It is not part of some new translation. It's not part of a New Age conspiracy to promote oneness, nor is it in need of a metaphysical interpretation. This Scripture has been present in the Bible for centuries. What's vitally important is how we make meaning of it and live out the Scripture in our daily lives.

Consider 1 Corinthians 12:12-13 (NIV):

> *Just as a body, though one, has many parts, but all its many parts form one body, so it is with Christ. For we were all baptized by one Spirit so as to form one body—whether Jews or Gentiles, slave or free—and we were all given the one Spirit to drink.*

The Scripture has significant implications for the equal standing of all men and women—Christian men and women specifically. For those who consider themselves to be Christians, Christ is the point at which we recognize the full presence of God in each other, regardless of labels such as race, ethnicity or gender. Inclusively interpreted, though we may show up on this planet as men and women, respectively, we each are equally vital to the whole.

And to end with the Scripture we started with, consider again Genesis 1:27 (NLT).

So God created human beings in his own image, in the image of God he created them, male and female he created them.

The three aforementioned Scriptures suggest no specific roles for men or women in God's kingdom. They do not imply superiority or inferiority, nor do they relegate anyone to the status of *other*. Adherence to these Scriptures will diminish the oppression and violence that women incur from men who believe the world is theirs. In the new world, religious rules, dogma and indoctrination take a backseat to the transformative power of Christ.

JESUS AS FEMINIST AND CHRIST CONSCIOUSNESS

Jesus' words and actions toward women in the Scriptures are nothing short of revolutionary. Jesus always defied the social norms of his time. Sarah Bessey, author of *Jesus Feminist: An Invitation To Revisit The Bible's View of Women*, reminds us that whether it was the Samaritan woman at the well, the prostitute, adulteress or the mentally ill, He never spoke to women through the lens of superiority or patriarchy. When the woman with the issue of blood reached out to touch the hem of His garment, He praised her faith and healed her. When the woman caught in adultery faced stoning, He protected her, invited her into the glory of grace, and dismissed her accusers by writing in the sand. In a time when a woman's word was worthless, Mary Magdalene was the first witness to Christ's resurrection; thereby becoming the first preacher of the resurrection.

> *"We can miss the crazy beauty of it because of the lack of fanfare in Scripture. Women were simply there, part of the revolution of love, sometimes unnamed, sometimes in the background, sometimes the receiver, sometimes the giver—just like every other man in Scripture, to be engaged on their own merit in the midst of their own story. Jesus thinks women are people, too."*[5]

The words and deeds of Jesus are supposed to be the Christian's example. We share in the Christ consciousness that spawned Jesus' actions. If we, as men, will allow God to free us of the patriarchal mind, we can then adopt the Christ mind—where conflict and violence related to duality is nonexistent.

I will end this chapter as I started, with two Scriptures taken from *The Inclusive Bible*, created by Priests for Equality in the effort to produce a more inclusive, non-sexist text. Both Scriptures offer a depiction of the creation stories found in the book of Genesis. The inclusive nature of the language provides alternative images that can heal the divide that traditional language often causes in the minds of many Christians. Consider Genesis 1:26-27 and Genesis 2:21-23 from The Inclusive Bible: First Egalitarian Translation:

---

5. Sarah Bessey, *Jesus Feminist: An Invitation to Revisit the Bible's View of Women* (New York: Howard Books, 2013), 22.

Then God said, "Let us make humankind in our image, to be like us. Let them be stewards of the fish in the sea, the birds of the air, the cattle, the wild animals, and everything that crawls on the ground."

Humankind was created as God's reflection: in the divine image God created them; female and male, God made them.

Genesis 1:26-27

So YHWH made the earth creature fall into a deep sleep, and while it slept, God divided the earth creature in two, then closed up the flesh from its side. YHWH then fashioned the two halves into male and female, and presented them to one another. When the male realized what had happened, he exclaimed, "This time, this is the one! Bone of my bone, and flesh of my flesh! Now, she will be Woman, and I will be Man, because We are of one flesh!"

Genesis 2:21-23

The two Scriptures above, inclusively translated, produce vastly different images of God and women. In the first Scripture, we imagine a God who creates humankind without denoting a separation of *man* and *woman*. The second Scripture implies a more egalitarian relationship between man and woman due to a less subordinate depiction of woman's creation. With the use of inclusive language as the norm, rather than the exception, we can begin the process of creating a society where patriarchy and masculinity cease to eclipse humanity.

CHAPTER 7
FINAL THOUGHTS

WHEN I BEGAN my studies at New York Theological Seminary, I had no idea how the study of Conflict Transformation would alter the course of my life. The one thing I knew when I started the program was that I had a desire to evolve into a more compassionate human being. It was my hope that this would inspire me to be a better husband—one who wasn't afraid to love, to be vulnerable, and to be present. In turn, I wanted to use these newfound skills to help others eliminate violence and foster peace in their relationships. My journey provided me much more than I bargained for. What I initially thought would be a study of the behavioral changes men could make to reduce violence toward women became an in-depth analysis of the roots of that violence—including men's longstanding perceptions of women, themselves, and the programming that undergirds those perceptions.

I currently teach life skills courses to men in DeKalb County Jail, located in Decatur, GA. The curriculum, or process, that I use, *Uncover, Recover, Discover* ©, is one that I developed based on the evolving nature of my own life. The idea is that to transform our lives, we must bring to light what has previously been hidden. We must forgive and reconcile our past, then discover, or *re*discover, our ability to create and *re*create the circumstances of our lives, rather than becoming victims of happenstance. There is no escaping the process for those who desire authentic, long-term transformation. I was certainly no exception. I had to begin *uncovering* by acknowledging that my perception of the tension that characterized many of my intimate relationships was skewed by the lens in which I saw through. Having no in-depth knowledge of the concepts and effects of patriarchy and hyper-masculinity, I began to consider that my relationships with women had been clouded by this lens. It became apparent that my course of study, Conflict Transformation, was perfectly suited for me. Staying true to its concepts, I decided to immerse myself in the tension rather than run away from it. In doing so, I developed the courage to bring *clarity* to my past and *presence* to the now moments—knowing that my future will be dictated by how well I do those two things.

> *"He who passively accepts evil is as much involved in it as he who helps to perpetrate it. He who accepts evil without protesting against it is really cooperating with it."*
>
> *—Martin Luther King, Jr.*

To dismiss the work it takes to transform oneself into a more loving, compassionate and empathetic human being is to be complicit in the ills of society. Those who choose to ignore the sexist, racist, homophobic, and other hate-filled elements present in society are often those who benefit from it. For much of my life, I was complicit in the oppression of women because I did not want to *see* it. I had the privilege of not *seeing* it. My resistance to acknowledge how I contributed to the pain of women in my personal life contributed to my tendency to turn a blind eye to the oppression of women the world over. The process of *seeing* required me to remove all the barriers within me that prevented me from feeling the individual and collective pain of women. It required me to reconcile areas of my life that I had chosen to forget. It required me to forgive myself and request forgiveness for my sins of ignorance. It required a level of surrender that I hadn't previously known. It *was* and *is* a painful process; healing often is. But through that pain comes freedom, reconciliation and redemption.

I've heard it said that truth is found in the tension. I think to some extent, that's true. What I *know* to be true, though, is that truth can never be found if tension is avoided. Our community, country, and world will never move toward healing if we remain reluctant to face the pain of uncovering what we'd rather keep hidden. The process of reconciliation cannot begin until we become unafraid to walk into that dark place that holds the secrets that have kept us sick. When we can stand with each other in that place, without moving, flinching, or allowing guilt and shame to make us flee, our humanity will slowly be revealed, and the masks that have marked our tribalism will begin to fall off. *This* is Conflict Transformation.

Author and philosopher Edmund Burke once said, "The only thing necessary for the triumph of evil is for good men to do nothing." I am not one who believes in, or focuses on, the power of evil. Regardless of what's happening in the world, I choose to wake up each morning and see the inherent good in men *and* women. And regardless of appearances, I choose to believe that good will always triumph over evil. I believe that if you have read this book, you are one of the good ones. If that be the case, the only thing left to do is to put the book down and get busy *doing something*.

BIBLIOGRAPHY

Adams, Carol J., and Marie M. Fortune, eds. *Violence Against Women and Children: A Christian Theological Sourcebook.* New York: Continuum, 1995.

Anderson, Cheryl B. *Ancient Laws and Contemporary Controversies: The Need for Inclusive Biblical Interpretation.* Oxford: Oxford University Press, 2009.

Augsburger, David W. *Conflict Mediation across Cultures: Pathways and Patterns.* Louisville, KY: Westminster/John Knox Press, 1992.

Bachman, Ronet, and Linda Saltzman. "Violence against Women: Estimates from the Redesigned Survey." *Bureau of Justice Statistics Report,* August 1995. http://www.bjs.gov/content/pub/pdf/FEMVIED.PDF.

Beauvoir, Simone de. *The Second Sex.* New York: Vintage, 2011.

Bentz, Valerie Malhotra, and Jeremy J. Shapiro. *Mindful Inquiry in Social Research.* Thousand Oaks, CA: Sage, 1998.

Bessey, Sarah. *Jesus Feminist: An Invitation to Revisit the Bible's View of Women.* New York: Howard Books, 2013.

Bradshaw, John. *Healing the Shame That Binds You.* Deerfield Beach, FL: Health Communications, 2005.

Brown, Robert McAfee. *Religion and Violence.* 2nd ed. Philadelphia: Westminster Press, 1987.

Brownmiller, Susan. *Against Our Will: Men, Women, and Rape.* New York: Fawcett Books, 1993.

Buchwald, Emilie, Pamela R. Fletcher, and Martha Roth, eds. *Transforming a Rape Culture.* Rev. ed. Minneapolis: Milkweed Editions, 2005.

Bush, Robert A. Baruch, and Joseph P. Folger. *The Promise of Mediation: The Transformative Approach to Conflict.* San Francisco: Jossey-Bass, 2005.

Carter, Jimmy. "Losing My Religion for Equality." *The Age,* July 15, 2009. http://www.theage.com.au/federal-politics/losing-my-religion-for-equality-20090714-dkov.html.

———. *A Call to Action: Women, Religion, Violence, and Power.* New York: Simon & Schuster, 2014.

Cone, James H. *God of the Oppressed.* Rev. ed. Maryknoll, N.Y.: Orbis Books, 1997.

Connell, Raewyn. *Masculinities.* 2nd ed. Berkeley: University of California Press, 2005.

Cooper-White, Pamela. *The Cry of Tamar: Violence Against Women and the Church's Response.* 2nd ed. Minneapolis: Fortress Press, 2012.

Daly, Mary. *Beyond God the Father: Toward a Philosophy of Women's Liberation.* Boston: Beacon Press, 1985.

DeConick, April D. *Holy Misogyny: Why the Sex and Gender Conflicts in the Early Church Still Matter.* New York: Bloomsbury Academic, 2013.

Dutton, Donald G., and Susan K. Golant. *The Batterer: A Psychological Profile.* Princeton, NJ: Recording for the Blind & Dyslexic, 2004.

Freire, Paulo. *Pedagogy of the Oppressed.* Rev. ed. London: Penguin Books, 1996.

———. *Pedagogy of Freedom: Ethics, Democracy, and Civic Courage.* Lanham, MD: Rowman & Littlefield, 1998.

Graff, Gerald, and Carole Birkenstein. *They Say I Say: The Moves That Matter in Academic Writing.* 2nd ed. New York: W. W. Norton & Co., 2010.

Hatty, Suzanne. *Masculinities, Violence and Culture.* Sage Series On Violence Against Women. Thousand Oaks, CA: Sage Publications, 2000.

Henderson, Jim. *The Resignation of Eve: What If Adam's Rib Is No Longer Willing to Be the Church's Backbone?* Carol Stream, IL: BarnaBooks, 2012.

hooks, bell. *We Real Cool: Black Men and Masculinity.* New York: Routledge, 2004.

———. *The Will to Change: Men, Masculinity, and Love.* New York: Washington Square Press, 2004.

———. *Outlaw Culture.* London: Routledge, 2006.

Jhally, Sut. *Dreamworlds. Desire, Sex and Power in Music Videos.* Northampton, MA: Media Education Foundation, 2007.

Johnson, Allan G. *The Gender Knot: Unraveling Our Patriarchal Legacy.* Rev. ed. Philadelphia: Temple University Press, 2005.

———. *Privilege, Power, and Difference.* 2nd ed. Boston: McGraw-Hill, 2006.

Jung, C. G. *Aspects of the Masculine.* Translated by John Beebe. Princeton, NJ: Princeton University Press, 1989.

Jung, Patricia Beattie, Aana Marie Vigen, and John Anderson, eds. *God, Science, Sex, Gender: An Interdisciplinary Approach to Christian Ethics.* Urbana: University of Illinois Press, 2010.

Katz, Jackson. *The Macho Paradox: Why Some Men Hurt Women and How All Men Can Help.* Naperville, IL: Sourcebooks, 2006.

———. "Violence against Women-It's a Men's Issue." Lecture, TED Channel, San Francisco, CA, November 2012. http://www.youtube.com/watch?v=ElJxUVJ8blw. Accessed September 12, 2013.

Kimmel, Michael S. "Searching for a New Boyhood: The Testosterone vs. Feminism Debate." *Voice Male: The Magazine of the Men's Resource Center of Western Massachusetts* (Winter 2000): 8-10.

———. *Manhood in America: A Cultural History.* 3rd ed. New York: Oxford University Press, 2012.

———. *Angry White Men: American Masculinity at the End of an Era.* New York: Nation Books, 2013.

King, Martin Luther, Jr. "Loving Your Enemies." Sermon delivered at Dexter Avenue Baptist Church, Montgomery, Alabama, November 17, 1957.

Knight, Jennie S. *Feminist Mysticism and Images of God: A Practical Theology.* St. Louis, MO: Chalice Press, 2011.

Kristof, Nicholas D., and Sheryl Wu Dunn. *Half the Sky: Turning Oppression Into Opportunity for Women Worldwide.* New York: Vintage Books, 2010.

Law, Eric H. F. *Inclusion: Making Room for Grace.* St. Louis, MO: Chalice Press, 2000.

Lederach, John Paul. *The Little Book of Conflict Transformation.* Intercourse, PA: Good Books, 2003.

Means, Patrick. *Men's Secret Wars.* Grand Rapids, MI: Fleming H. Revell, 1999.

Miedzian, Myriam. *Boys Will Be Boys: Breaking the Link between Masculinity and Violence.* New York: Lantern Books, 2002.

Miles, Al. *Domestic Violence: What Every Pastor Needs to Know.* 2nd ed. Minneapolis: Fortress Press, 2011.

National Center for Injury Prevention and Control. *Costs of Intimate Partner Violence Against Women in the United States.* Atlanta, GA: Centers for Disease Control and Prevention, National Centers for Injury Prevention and Control, 2003. http://www.cdc.gov/violenceprevention/pdf/IPVBook-a.pdf.

Patterson, Orlando. *Rituals of Blood: Consequences of Slavery in Two American Centuries.* Washington, DC: Civitas/CounterPoint, 1998.

Paulk, D. E. *The Holy Bible of Inclusion.* Atlanta, GA: Cathedral of the Holy Spirit, 2011.

Pearson, Carlton. *The Gospel of Inclusion: Reaching Beyond Religious Fundamentalism to the True Love of God.* New York: Atria, 2008.

Poling, James N. *The Abuse of Power: A Theological Problem.* Nashville, TN: Abingdon Press, 1991.

Rennison, Callie Marie. "Intimate Partner Violence, 1993-2001." *Bureau of Justice Statistics Crime Data Brief,* February 2003. http://www.bjs.gov/content/pub/pdf/ipv01.pdf.

Robinson, Lori. *I Will Survive: The African-American Guide to Healing from Sexual Assault and Abuse.* New York: Seal Press, 2002.

Ruether, Rosemary Radford. *Sexism and God-Talk: Toward a Feminist Theology*. Boston: Beacon Press, 1993

Sanday, Peggy Reeves. *Fraternity Gang Rape: Sex, Brotherhood, and Privilege On Campus*. 2nd ed. New York: New York University Press, 2007.

Southern Baptist Convention. "Position Statements: Women in Ministry." http://www.sbc.net/aboutus/positionstatements.asp.

Spong, John Shelby. *The Sins of Scripture: Exposing the Bible's Texts of Hate to Reveal the God of Love*. San Francisco: HarperSanFrancisco, 2005.

Stone, Merlin. *When God Was a Woman*. New York: Harcourt Brace Jovanovich, 1978.

Swidler, Leonard J. *Jesus Was a Feminist: What the Gospels Reveal About His Revolutionary Perspective*. Lanham, MD: Sheed & Ward, 2007.

Tarrant, Shira. *Men and Feminism*. Berkeley, CA: Seal Press, 2009.

Tate, Karen. *Voices of the Sacred Feminine*. Alresford, UK: John Hunt Publishing, 2014.

Tjaden, Patricia, and Nancy Thoennes. "Prevalence, Incidence, and Consequences of Violence Against Women." *National Institute of Justice Centers for Disease Control and Prevention, Research in Brief*, November 1998. https://www.ncjrs.gov/pdffiles/172837.pdf.

———. *Extent, Nature and Consequences of Intimate Partner Violence: Findings for the National Violence Against Women Survey*. Washington, DC: National Institute of Justice and the Centers of Disease Control and Prevention, July 2000. https://www.ncjrs.gov/pdffiles1/nij/181867.pdf.

Toomey, Michele. "The Price of Masculinity Based on Violence." *Education Digest* 58, no. 4 (1992): 44-46.

Vision Forum Ministries. "The Tenets of Biblical Patriarchy." https://homeschoolersanonymous.files.wordpress.com/2014/04/the-tenets-of-biblical-patriarchy-vision-forum-ministries.pdf (accessed April 24, 2016).

Winslade, John, and Gerald Monk. *Narrative Mediation: A New Approach to Conflict Resolution*. San Francisco: Jossey-Bass, 2000.

ABOUT THE AUTHOR

S PENCER A. MURRAY is Co-Founder and Visionary Partner of *Off-Script*, LLC., a relationship development company. He is a former educator with the Detroit Public Schools where he taught at **Paul Robeson Academy**, an *African-Centered School*; and the **Academy of the Americas**, a *Dual Language Immersion School*. He attended **Western Michigan University** where he received a Bachelor's Degree and a Master of Arts Degree in Educational Leadership. While serving as an elementary and middle school teacher, he attained an advanced degree in Teaching from **Wayne State University**. He furthered his studies by later receiving his Doctor of Ministry Degree from **New York Theological Seminary**, where his focus of study was **Conflict Transformation**. His doctoral work focused on the systematic influence of patriarchy in society, and its tendency to oppress and perpetrate violence towards women. This work has led him to work with men and boys as it relates to unhealthy ideas of masculinity and how these ideas contribute to violence towards self, women, and community. In addition to conducting healthy relationship workshops, he and his wife, Erica, facilitate *OffScript Conversations: Race.Relationships.Reconciliation,* in an effort to promote racial understanding and harmony. His commitment to service has also led him to do work with the **Ben Marion Institute for Social Justice**, the **National Center for Civil and Human Rights**, the **Junior League of Atlanta**, and the **Urban League of Greater Atlanta**. He currently teaches transformational courses to men at the **DeKalb County Sheriff's Office**. His years of experience working with boys and men, as well as his own struggle to free himself from the prison of toxic masculinity, drives his passion to lead men to a deeper understanding of themselves; an understanding that is characterized by a healthy respect for women, and a reverence for the feminine aspect of creation.

Made in the USA
Coppell, TX
01 June 2023

17588961R00059